STOPWATCH TEACHER

Edith Coffin Robertson

ISBN 978-0-9727721-3-6

© Copyright 2007
by
Edith Coffin Robertson

cover photography by
Alicia Robertson

Robertson Publishing
59 N. Santa Cruz Avenue, Suite B
Los Gatos, California 95030 USA
(888) 354-5957 • www.RobertsonPublishing.com

Also by Edith Robertson

Life on a Missouri Farm
Autobiography of Edith Coffin

Recollections of a Long and Interesting Life, Vol I

Recollections of a Long and Interesting Life, Vol II

Stopwatch Teacher

RECOLLECTIONS

	Introduction	i
	Prologue - I Did It My Way	iii
1.	Edith Tells About Edith	1
2.	Stopwatch Teaching	7
3.	April Fool's Day	13
4.	Glen and the Pop-up Quiz	17
5.	Teaching & Learning	20
6.	An Athlete I'm Not	30
7.	Control	36
8.	Control - Good and Bad	40
9.	Substitute Teaching	43
10.	A Full Time Teacher	48
11.	Supercalifragilisticexpialidocious	52
12.	Fourth Grader Jerry	57
13.	Reading for Recreation	60
14.	Teaching at Lone Hill School	64
15.	Jack LaLanne and I	69
16.	Union of Union	73
17.	Teaching Outside the Book	77
18.	Strong Teacher Needed	93
19.	Chip and the Pearls	99
20.	Friend Sammy	100
21.	Teacher Effectiveness	103
22.	A Friday in the Life of Edith	109
23.	My Kind of Teaching	117
24.	Vineland Gathering	121
25.	California Again… and Again… and Again	125
26.	Epilogue	129

I am writing to make sense out of my years. I've done the best I could, but some names and details in my writings have been altered. And, since my teaching years went from September to September it is impossible to say, "This happened in this particular year," for every chronological year.

This book grew in the telling—my diaries date back over seventy years and I keep adding to them. As such, I am publishing my recollections in several volumes; the one you're holding now is a special edition of teaching-related chapters from the first two volumes of my autobiography, *Recollections of a Long and Interesting Life*.

This book was suggested by Dr. James Asher, an educator who appreciates innovative teaching. I hope you enjoy the stories as much as I did the living of them. ECR

PROLOGUE

Finally, I could start teaching! I had received my teaching degree in 1937. Twenty years is a long time to wait. But finally, 1957, with my youngest child Jonathan in Kindergarten, I was ready. Well, not really ready. I decided to take a few refresher classes.

"Pipe the D-A-R," a young university gal whispered to her friend. I thought she was referring to my advanced age, calling me a *Daughter of the American Revolution*. Fifty-three was a bit old to be enrolled in teacher training. But no, she had meant "a damned average raiser." Never mind. Young snippit! She'll be fifty-three some day and she won't think she's too old to be important. I whizzed through that course then took a few other teacher-training courses.

Then, my first class, a fourth grade. My aim: teach the basics as prescribed by the board of education and make it fun for the kids. And how did I do that? I resolved to forget most of the college training classes. I'd do it my way. I printed my motto in capital letters in my grade book: **IF THEY AIN'T LEARNED IT, I AIN'T TAUGHT IT.**

I changed techniques to fit different kids. When Danny balked at folk dancing, saying he wanted to be a priest and "should not touch a woman," I got help from his priest.

When Manuel beat me in a chess game I realized his IQ on the school records had to be wrong. We stayed after school for special coaching until he caught up.

I tried my best, year after year, to bring the kids up to grade level. What a challenge. Their reading levels as school started in September ranged from first grade to high school level. My job was to get them ready for the fifth grade. Some kids had given up. I told them, over and over, my mother had convinced the school that I should repeat the first grade. I'd remind some of the boys, "No one bats a thousand."

I sometimes pitted girls against boys, sometimes blue eyes against brown eyes (it would be years later before I'd learn that that might not have been such a great idea), or those who had a sweetheart against those who said their mother was their sweetheart. I used the stopwatch constantly.

The kids knew they would have to write almost every day. They also knew they would sometimes be expected to stand and read to the class. I kept constantly, in the back of my mind, my husband Ray's distress when he had to speak before a group. He resented getting through school with an A average and never learning to get up before a group. In Ray's mind, his teachers had failed to do their jobs. From time to time, during my teaching career, Ray would ask, "Are you getting those kids up before the class?"

Yes, I was following my husband's advice. Doing it my way, of course. On a typical writing period I might say, "Just ten minutes today. Notebook open. Pencil in hand. Eyes closed. Think of what you had for breakfast. Open eyes. Write!" Then I'd call time and tell them to count the words. They'd put the total at the end of their writing and try to do better the next time. Sometimes I'd ask for volunteers to read what they'd written, but the kids knew their writing was private; I never read what they wrote and no one had to share. Jerry stood with notebook open, only a few sentences there, glibly pretended to share what he had written, but I never called his bluff.

I tried to make them want to write. Subject matter could range from "Why I Hate Boys (Girls)" to "My Best Vacation." One of their favorite subjects was "What I Don't Like About Teachers."

I made friends with the parents. I played ball with the kids. One of our favorite games on rainy days was "Screwy Louie." We arranged the desks in two sections facing each other, and tied a rope fairly high to indicate the top of a net. The inside of an old volleyball we used was too soft to do damage as it bounced off walls and windows. The kids had to stay seated and every volley was fair unless it bounced off the ceiling. The kids quickly learned volleyball rotation as they hotly contested each point. They sometimes laughed so loud other kids would leave their own rooms where they had been playing checkers or dominos to stand at the back of our room, to watch and cheer.

It was the fourth grade teacher's job to review adding and subtracting facts (this meant a re-teaching process) and then go on and help the kids learn the multiplication and division facts. I bought records of the facts in syncopated rhythm for the kids to sing to. We worked to have each kid master all the multiplication and division facts with 98% to 100% accuracy in a 100 item two-minute test. When each had accomplished this he'd be excused early at recess time. In addition, those who had mastered the facts were allowed to play chess on Fridays while the other kids drilled with flash cards.

I somehow knew that the standard model for teaching didn't work; in my opinion, a teacher droning away at the front of a class of students taking notes isn't teaching much of anything. Kids learn better when they're active and having fun, and we all learn best through active participation.

In short, I didn't teach the way other teachers did or even the way I'd been taught in college; I did what worked for me and my students. And when that failed (as it sometimes did), I changed my tactics. I learned as I taught, and tried not to repeat mistakes. I was unorthodox. I did it my way.

STOPWATCH TEACHER

Edith Tells about Edith

My mama and daddy lived on an Oklahoma farm. They had a two-year-old boy, Wilbur, and my mama, Edith, wanted a pretty baby girl. May 29, 1914 Mama tried desperately to push me out into the world. Ione, my Mama's sister, stood by with encouragement. Daddy drove to Shawnee, the nearest town, to let Dr. Hughes know he'd be needed in a few hours. However, it was not just a few hours. Edith travailed in pain hour after weary hour. That baby was stuck in the birth canal. Finally Dr. Hughes took the birth forceps, reached in to get a good grip on the baby's head, and delivered the squalling infant. He cleaned off the worst of the mess, and held up the baby, "Well, you got your little girl, Edie, and she's a husky—eleven pounds."

Mama looked at my pulled-out-of-shape head, and gasped, "It's a monster! Look at the head! Oh, God, how can you allow this to happen?" She turned her back on the doctor and sobbed in horror and grief.

"There, there," old Dr. Hughes said, "She's going to be all right. I'll just push her head back into shape. You'll see." His big old hands pushed and prodded at my head. Edith kept on crying, refusing to look at her new baby. When she woke she regained her composure, took the little one to nurse, and as the child suckled, said, "Hello, little Edith Junior. Welcome to the Brookover family. You have a pretty face and I expect soon your brown hair will grow long. It looks like it's going to be curly. No one will ever know the back of your head is flat."

Well, as Mama said, it is a good thing my hair is curly. Only the hairdresser knows the shape I'm in.

Later we had five more girls. With a big family Daddy and Mama worked hard on the farm but they couldn't make it and we moved to Shawnee. Daddy put a big sign in his car and a cardboard sign on his hat that said "Taxi." He was a favorite with the Indians because he didn't cheat them.

But times were hard in the Great Depression days so Daddy and Mama made a really big move when I was a third grader. Daddy drove the truck and Mama, beside him, held baby LaVerne. Wilbur, Ruth, Lela, Babbie and I got to ride on the mattresses in back. We were going to California. Daddy stopped often so we could work. We had long canvas sacks over one shoulder, and went up and down rows picking cotton. One day I picked as much cotton as Wilbur, 100 pounds.

In Cotati, north of San Francisco, Daddy started a chicken farm. That was hard work, and we stayed very poor. When Dorothea was born we had nine in the family. We wore hand-me-down clothes. Mama watered the milk to make it go around. Mama went to get free food for the poor and cried inside when people make sarcastic remarks about her big family.

Many people tried to help. Uncle Joe gave Mama money for doing his laundry. I was hired at $10.00 a month to be the church custodian. Cousin Velma gave me her outgrown clothes. Daddy kept yelling about how much we ate and how we ought to drop out of school and go to work.

"So they can be poor chicken farmers?" Mama asked. "The only way out of poverty is through education."

When I was a seventh grader, I was sent to work for my board and room. I cleaned house, cared for the small children, and cooked. I worked for board and room all the way through junior high and high school. Life wasn't easy. It was no fun to be the "hired girl," but I learned how other people lived and, away from my dad, no one was begrudging me every bite I ate. I had no social life but I had plenty of time to read and do my homework.

At last a way out of poverty came. In 1933, at the age of 19, I won the Petaluma High School PTA scholarship. With that start I worked my way through San Francisco State College, and earned a teaching credential. Once more I worked in homes but this time it wasn't a hopeless life sentence.

Many people befriended me. Two girl friends encouraged me in my Christian walk; many of my employers took an interest in the country bumpkin from the chicken farm.

The year 1937 was memorable. I was twenty-three. I married, graduated from college, moved to Los Gatos, and had a baby—all in that order. That wonderful man in my life, 32 year old Raymond Glen Robertson, was an accountant, businessman, and musician. He was brilliant, complicated, introverted, a devout Christian. And he was a very determined man. When he made up his mind, he acted. We met one month, were engaged the next, and married the next.

Marriage and rearing three children kept me occupied for a few years, but I'd worked hard all my life and had no intention to stop my busy lifestyle. I ran a boarding home for children for ten years and helped my husband in his various businesses: Polly Prim Bakery, Los Gatos Sewing Machines, and Los Gatos Office Equipment & Supply.

When the children were all in school, I finally used my teaching credential. I taught in the middle grades for twenty years in the Union School District.

After fifty years of up and down marriage (with far more ups than downs), my life partner became desperately ill. Dr. Ness put it to me bluntly, "Do you want to be a teacher, or do you want to be married? Ray needs you at home." As much as I loved teaching, I loved Ray more.

February 28, 1977, at the age of 62, I gave my friendly principal, Steve, one day's notice, and I was home the next day. I joined Ray in the home office and he began to teach me how to take over the books of Los Gatos Office Equipment. When he became seriously ill ten years later, I became Ray's caregiver.

Sheri, our daughter, moved in with us at that time, and she and our son Jon kept the business going. As Ray became weaker, my brother Wil came from Hawaii to help. January 24, 1987 was our fiftieth wedding anniversary, but there was no celebration. Ray was too ill to know and I was too tired to care.

Finally Ray set his mind to one more task. He said to Wil, sitting beside him, "Wil, when you have to do something you might as well make up your mind and just go ahead and do it." I returned from the drug store where I'd gone on the advice of the hospice nurse to get rubbing alcohol for Ray. My brother looked up.

"You won't need the alcohol, Sis. Ray's gone." Ray died February 4, 1987.

Grieving is hard work but I finally worked my way back into an active life. I opened my home to renters to get some extra income. I hosted a church group monthly. I watched Ken, my ten-hour-a-month gardener, as he skillfully landscaped. Vicky came for a half day twice a month to do the house cleaning.

My three talented "kids" skillfully guided me in my widowhood journey. I am mother to three, grandmother to five, and great-grandmother to six. In my nineties, I say, "I am a 'Cotton Picking Oakie,' not retired—just re-fired."

My love for Jesus, my Lord and Savior, is the controlling force of my life. My church is of upmost importance to me. Weekly Church and Sunday School attendance and two weekly Bible studies give me guidance. A series on *Self-Confrontation* was instructive and humbling. *Forty Days of Purpose* inspired me.

I was an aide in reading instruction for first graders, then with fourth graders, in Los Gatos Christian School for six years, working from 9:00 to 11:00 a.m. five days a week. My guide teacher was a marvel. I wish, those twenty years I taught, that I'd been half as effective as she is. She works on the positive approach, is firm yet loving.

For sheer unadulterated fun, try working with first graders. They are delightful. One went home and said to his mom, "I have a grandma teacher. I don't know her name but she's a grandma teacher."

Later I went for only a half hour daily, tried to teach the kids how to write their life story. The time allowed me was not enough. After struggling to fit the lesson into such a short time I had to call it quits, so that ended my teaching career.

It was time. I was almost 89 years old. *So now what?* Write my memoirs, of course! ✎

Stopwatch Teaching

When I was boarding children I found a kitchen timer very helpful. When there was an argument, "He won't give me my turn," I'd settle things by bringing out the timer. Kids respect the impersonality of a timer; it shows no favoritism.

Bedtime was always dreaded but accepted when the timer told just how many minutes were left before the lights were out.

I brought my kitchen timer with me when I started teaching. The school authorities set times for each subject. One hour was the usual time for reading. Since we grouped for reading and exchanged students it was no problem to keep to the reading time. Forty minutes for arithmetic, twenty minutes for penmanship. Other subjects varied. I loved teaching language arts. It was easy to get carried away and take time from arithmetic when things were going well. I posted a big time schedule. That was a help but the time problems finally were solved when I had the kids take turns being official timekeeper.

The official timekeeper had permission to stand as a signal to me that it was one minute 'til time to change to the next subject. What fun to boss the teacher! Of course, no timekeeper ever let me forget it was time for physical education. And always Steve would prompt the timekeeper when it was close to math time. That boy didn't like to read but how he did love arithmetic. Various kids had favorite subjects and so we were kept on schedule.

A Dirty Trick

Then I bought a stopwatch to help in the math period. State standards at that time for fourth graders: 100 mixed multiplication or division facts in four minutes. We drilled with flash cards, had teams, played games, and listened to syncopated math music, held contests, posted charts of improvement.

I played a dirty trick on each class at the beginning of the year. I'd give a paper with 100 ever-so-easy math facts (1+1, 2+2, 5+5, 10+10, etc.) and showed the kids the stopwatch. I posted times on the front chalkboard as each child finished. They were laughing with delight when they saw their times.

Then I told them, "Now you know how fast you can write answers when you really know the facts. Soon you'll be doing 7x8 and 8x6 just as fast." They groaned at the mean trick I'd pulled on them. But, actually, all of the kids could score 100% in 4 minutes and most of the kids got 100% correct in only 2 minutes before the year was up.

Kids in Action

We used the stopwatch continually. The kids loved it when it was their week to be "Stopwatch Monitor." They would take the box with great pride, sign their names inside the box lid, wear the watch on its chain around their necks, call out loud and clear, "Start!" or "Time's up!" many times during the day. No one seemed to mind, as they knew each would get a turn.

Those kids would have made "Cheaper by the Dozen" jealous. They timed how fast they could get into alphabetical order and pass in their papers. They timed how fast they could come in from recess and get seated and ready for class. As soon as they set a record they would plan to break it.

That stopwatch was one of the most valuable teaching devices of my twenty-year's teaching career.

Jon came from work to my schoolroom at Vineland one day to adjust my television. The fourth graders were very interested in watching him up on the ladder in the front of the room, making the adjustments. Sheila was thrilled. She murmured in great satisfaction, "O-o-h, a business man!"

On the other hand, Jon was interested as he took notice of my teaching techniques. He advised me when I was writing the memoirs, "I never had a teacher who taught your way. Don't forget to write how you had the kids trained with the stopwatch. "

Editor's Comment

Jon speaking. As Edith's former television fixer upper, I feel moved to relate that particular occasion from a slightly different perspective. True, I had come to fix the television; my mother was an innovator, and she was one of the first teachers to use television—which was high on a shelf overlooking the classroom. Which is where I found myself perched that day in my three piece suit and tie, twiddling knobs and wiggling antenna wires. It took far less time to make the picture look right than I had allowed; I was watching Edith's classroom from a unique vantage point of happenstance, looking down over the entire class.

There was a spelling test going on. Obviously a spelling test because the girl at the front of the class would say a word, then the kids would write, and then she'd say another word, the kids would write, and so on until the end. Which is when she called out *"FRONT!"* and every kid in that class scrambled out of their desk, bumped and jumbled their way to the middle row and somehow made themselves into a single file, from the front of the class to the back. At which point the last kid in line handed his paper to the kid in front of him. And that kid took it, added his own paper, and handed both to the next kid. Et cetera, over and over until the kid in the front of the line handed the entire stack to the girl who'd been giving the test. Who took them over to my mother's desk (Edith never looked up, she was working on something), but then came back to the front and stood there for a second, after which she said *"GO!"* and all the kids scrambled and bumped and jostled their way back to their seats as if their lives depended on it. At which point the girl in front said *"DONE!"* and whipped her arm in a circle again and then went to the blackboard and wrote something with a bit of chalk and then sat down. And then my mother stood up, came to the front of the class, and started to teach again. At which point I managed to put my eyes back in their parent sockets and get down the ladder and stagger over to the door. I motioned Edith I was leaving, and she followed me out.

"What was all *that?*" I asked, as we walked towards the parking lot.

"You mean the spelling test?" She really didn't know what I was talking about.

"No. I could see it was a spelling test! I mean all the rest of it—the kids in the line and the arm waving and so on." I looked at my mother. She did look like my mother. Same eyes, same hair and all that, but this was her bailiwick and I was no longer her son — but rather a grown man who happened to be her son, seeing her with different eyes.

"Oh *that.*" she said. She looked at me. "You mean all the other stuff that went on."

"Yes. All the other stuff." We were standing by the car.

"Well, the school district doesn't pay me a high salary to give spelling tests," she explained, "so I always have the kid who got the most right last time give it the next time. That way I can spend my time doing something useful, like prepping for the next lesson.

"Well, the district doesn't pay me to sort papers, either," she added. "But many teachers put the kids in alphabetical order, and I teach fourth grade."

"Okay..."

"Well, by the time they get to me they've had three years of sitting in the middle of the same four classmates, and they've gotten to know each other, and they're too comfortable and they aren't learning anymore. The real problem is that the ones who need my attention are sometimes in the back and the ones who are used to being called on all the time are always in the middle — so I mix it up a bit."

I must have given her a look, because she labored on.

"Yes, well. You see, I have this theory. My theory is that with fourth graders, their heinies are connected to their brains. And if they sit for longer than twenty minutes at a time, they go brain dead." She smiled at me. "And so I take every excuse I can think of to get them out of their seats on a regular basis. And I like to use contests because it makes it more fun."

"Contests?" I asked.

"Sure," she said. "The girl who was giving the test waved her arm because she had a stopwatch in her hand; she was clicking it. And the kids were lining up in alphabetical order so that when the papers got to my desk I wouldn't have to waste time re-ordering them."

"And what the girl wrote on the blackboard was the time it took them to do all this, right?"

"Right. It was a score. They get points out of it." She was smiling, and I think I was, too.

It's a rather wonderful awakening to know all of a sudden at the age of whatever that you have had this terribly bright and capable mom all your life, even though you didn't really know it at the time. ✍

April Fool's Day

A brown haired woman stands outside Room 14, the fourth grade classroom, one bright April morning. Putting her ear up against the scarred yellow door, she listens intently. Strange to hear nothing. She shrugs, knocks briefly, and then quietly enters, with the visitor's pass in her hand. A boy meets her and takes the pass. "My name is Mrs. Davis," she whispers. "I have come to observe."

"I am the greeter. Welcome to our class." He shows her a chair toward the back of the room, then puts the pass on the teacher's desk and returns quickly to his desk. He grabs his pencil and starts to work. What an industrious kid! How strange to have the room so quiet. Kyle said things got really loud at times.

But where is the teacher? And why are the kids so quiet? When her Erin had been a fourth grader she had told her that Mrs. Robertson's class was sometimes very noisy. She looks about the room. That is a funny kind of a bulletin board up on the left wall. What a title! **I Seen Him When He Done It!** There is a vast assortment of bits of writings. The phrases and sentences, obviously cut or torn from a variety of writings, are pinned helter-skelter, many overlapping others. She grins. A kid, whose paper is posted up there, with a silly mistake highlighted, will not be likely to repeat the same mistake.

And there on the other wall is another large bulletin board, a gigantic enlarged map of Vineland School District. The title: **Need Help? Find a Friend!** Every kid's name is on a paper flag pinned to his place of residence. Easy to see why the kids have no excuse for not getting an assignment. And it is no wonder Kyle knows where every one of his classmates lives.

There are six rows of desks, five desks in each row. Every kid has a sheet of paper on his desk and is writing rapidly. No one is looking at the tall pig-tailed girl, standing with dignity in front of the class, holding a stopwatch in her hand. Ah, there is her Kyle in the second row, head down, scribbling as fast as the other kids.

Two boys toward the center of the room sigh in satisfaction, grin, and sit back in their chairs. The girl in front of the room frowns at their noise, but keeps her eyes glued to the stopwatch. Suddenly she shouts, "Time's up! Pencils down!"

"You sure that was two minutes?" asks a boy.

"Yes, I'm sure. Ready! Stand! Pass papers!"

She holds out her right hand, stopwatch ready. And again she clicks the stopwatch. Each kid stands, paper in hand, then goes quickly to a place around the perimeter of the room. They turn and move rapidly. One after another, they place their papers in a tray on the teacher's desk, and return to their seats.

When the last kid is seated, the girl up front announces, "All papers are in. Forty-five seconds!" Some of the kids glance back at Mrs. Davis to see if she is impressed. She is impressed. Forty-five seconds to get the papers passed in? Kyle had told her that the papers were always in alphabetical order. Yes, definitely impressed. But somewhat bewildered. Where is that teacher?

"Turn to page 74 in your math book," the tall girl directs. "Your homework will be problems one through eight. Extra credit if you do number nine and ten. I will collect your papers when you come to school tomorrow."

"Oh, that's not fair!" comes several protests. "You can't give homework." Every kid in the class swivels, eyes toward the far corner of the room. Then Mrs. Davis sees the teacher. She is sitting, partially hidden behind a screen, book in hand, apparently reading.

She looks up and nods casually. "But, of course. Norah's the teacher. Teachers give homework." She lowers her eyes to her book. The kids place their math books on the top left corner of their desks and wait. Norah sits down in an empty desk and a boy goes to the front of the room.

"Please take out your language books," he directs. Mrs. Davis moves her chair to sit beside Mrs. Robertson.

"I hadn't planned to stay very long but this looks like fun. Do you mind telling me what it is all about?"

"I do it every April Fool's Day. We plan several days in advance. I take time to give each prospective teacher lesson planning tips. Each kid teaches a subject or a portion of a subject. No one knows who will be in charge of each segment of the day. They keep their parts secret until their turn comes. I will admit they sometimes surprise me. Norah's the first kid who ever thought of giving homework. I'll not be surprised when she asks for the class book to record the grades after she corrects the papers tomorrow. Norah is quite a girl."

"Will my Kyle get to be a teacher?"

"Yes, he's scheduled for the last period. He will be in charge of the physical education period."

"Oh, that should be easy for him. He's a super baseball player."

"For April Fool's Day? No, we'll play jacks."

Glen and the Pop-up Quiz

"Why in world did you mark up your Bible so much?" asked Dan, Glen's new son-in-law. "I find great patches of red and also blue all through both the Old Testament and New Testament." Dan was referring to the Bible Glen had given him recently. "I can understand someone underlining favorite verses, but you've got huge areas colored, some a half page long."

"Oh, those were parts I'd marked to memorize."

"Marked to memorize? That much? There are colored patches in every book of the Bible!"

"Memory work has never been difficult for me and I did it when I was a high school kid for some contests we were in."

I remember how, many years ago, Glen and some of his friends from Los Gatos Calvary Church met on Saturday nights to study for the pop-up quizzes. And I remember how smug I felt when our pastor gave a part of an evening service to let the congregation see how well the kids were doing.

Pop-up quizzes were popular all over the nation for several years. They got that name because, to respond to a Bible question, the one who could "pop up" (jump to his feet) and start answering first got the point for his team. Kids in church youth groups studied all year and took part in many practice drills on Saturday nights. They had to know the Bible very well but they also had to be very alert, quick to jump to their feet, and quick to respond. Contests between neighbor churches helped them prepare for the important final contests. The quizzes were nerve-wracking affairs, as hotly contested as football games.

That year, 1956, hundreds of high school kids from all over California crowded into the Montgomery Theater auditorium on Santa Clara Street in San Jose. Pastors, Sunday School teachers and parents were seated in the balcony. The contestants filled most of the downstairs area.

The kids sat, tense and eager, waiting. Pastor Davis introduced the quiz moderator who went over the rules for the benefit of the visitors. The kids all knew the rules, of course. They had been living with those rules (very simple but very rigid) several years as they drilled during their weekly meetings. They knew the slightest infraction would mean they were eliminated. Finally, the moderator turned to the kids. "Are you ready?"

"Yeah! Ready!" came the response. Each person was poised on the edge of his seat, ready to spring to his feet.

Pastor Davis started off with an easy one, pausing between each word, "In—the—beginning—"

A tall redheaded boy jumped up and rattled off, "In the beginning was the Word and the Word was with God and the Word was God —John 1:1."

Sadly Pastor Davis showed his sorrow while he shook his head. The boy moved to the back of the auditorium and sat down, out of the contest. Then Pastor Davis again said, even more slowly, "In—the—beginning—God—"

Another boy jumped up and shouted, "In the beginning God created the heavens and the earth —Genesis 1:1." Pastor Davis smiled and went on to the next quotation on his list.

As the kids were eliminated and moved to the back, the group of kids up front grew smaller and smaller. And the Bible references became more difficult, with verses such as: "Because you are lukewarm—" and "He who has an ear—" and "For the love of money—."

Glen was one of the six California finalists. I later used the Bible quiz method in my teaching for social studies. The kids sat forward in their seats, hands gripping the edges, ready to jump. I was very dramatic, and spoke ever so slowly. I said, "John—" and all my fourth graders sat still. They knew there were three men named John who were famous in California history. So I would repeat and go on "John Bid—" and some smart student would hop up out of his seat with "John Bidwell led the first covered wagon train into California before the Gold Rush."

The kids and I enjoyed the action. It was a good "show-off" activity for visitors. ✍

Teaching & Learning

I was ever so pleased when I was only four or five years old to have Mary, the "big" girl across the street come over and climb up in our big cottonwood tree with me and explain how to make doll blankets out of cottonwood leaves. We'd tear off leaves, remove the stems, and attach the leaves together using the stems as a pin.

"Do you want to learn how to make blankets out of leaves?" I asked Ruth, two years my junior. "First, I have to help you climb up in the tree." Ruth liked dolls and was eager to learn. I discovered it was fun to learn but even more delightful to teach.

Ruth listened to my bedtime stories with delight. I don't remember Lela or Babbie being in on our story time. They made a twosome of their own. Then we had our fifth girl, and Mama looked to me, eight years old, for help. By this time I was feeling very secure, loved taking baby sister LaVerne in my arms. Then as she grew older I often had

LaVerne straddled across one hip. We and the neighbor kids played with our bantam chickens, blew soap bubbles, did the usual kick-the-can and ball games. LaVerne and I were a unit. I was more a caregiver than a teacher at that age but I was definitely a manager of young ones.

When we were on our "Oakie-to-California" trip I was busy doing my bit to help Mama with the camp work. We all went out early to the cotton fields, dragging our long cotton sacks behind us. I related to Wilbur, my elder by two years, at this time. He could pick almost twice as much as I could yet somehow we often stayed in near-by rows of cotton. In the cotton-picking days I was more a learner than a teacher.

Our long trip ended in Pasadena, California, at the home of Dad's younger brother, Stanley. It looked as if all the dust bowl population had migrated to Pasadena. The schools went on triple shift. What confusion. My memory is just a vague mixture of coming and going to school. Mama must have been continually exhausted with her family of six kids, all the school age kids being fed at different times.

Mama's Helper

In 1929 we moved to Petaluma to live in the newly built chicken house at Grandma's. Living is a chicken house was an adventure. It had a bathroom at one end and a sort of kitchen at the other end with our living and sleeping area in between. Mama was expecting her seventh child and I was often in charge of the younger sisters. I was old enough to begin to learn how to cook. With eggs being free I naturally learned how to fry, boil and scramble eggs. I knew how to make deviled eggs, even how to color them purple with beet juice before cutting them open.

Mama taught me the complicated process of making bread. First, take the large dishpan. Roll up your sleeves, wash your hands. Put in eight large sifters of flour. Add two handfuls of sugar, a large hand scoop of shortening, a little salt and any leftover mashed potatoes. Crumble two cakes of yeast into the flour mixture; add just enough barely warm water to make a stiff dough. Mix the whole thing together. Dump the huge ball of dough out on a floured board, and knead it well. (I was so short that last part was hard and usually Mama took over.) Then put the dough in a greased pan, cover with a damp cloth and set it in a warm place till it gets twice as big.

I hadn't done the last part, yet, without Mama's help, of making the risen dough into loaves or rolls.

My life as a fourth grader was a pleasure. Good-natured, Irish, blue-eyed Miss Duggan was my teacher. I tried very hard to please her. March 29th Mama told me she was going to the hospital to have another baby and I was to be in charge of things as I was the oldest. I was pleased at the responsibility and felt very important as I looked about the kitchen, knowing I was in charge. I must have thrown my weight about a bit because Ruth rebelled. She got into my precious perfume and I became very angry. Then she really defied me. She went up to the rising dough Mama had to leave and poked her finger deep into the mass of rising dough. It went slowly down and I cried out in rage, "Now, look what you've done!

I left my responsibilities at home and ran the few blocks to the hospital to see Mama. Still in tears, I told her what Ruth had done. "Go home, Sis," Mama said gently, "By the time you get home the bread will have risen again. You will remember how we make it into loaves and how we bake it in the oven."

My Current Event

Fridays were "current event" days and I was distraught the morning after Mama had gone to the hospital, to realize I hadn't had time to prepare for my current event. I came through with flying colors, however, as I breathed deeply and announced: *"Last night Mrs.Brookover brought forth the smallest baby ever to born in the Petaluma Hospital. Her name is Dorothea and she has to live in an incubator because she came too soon and she is not finished yet."*

When Miss Duggan and I became friends years later she told me, "You can't imagine how your current event was a breath of fresh air to this bored teacher listening Friday after Friday as kids stumble over things they think of tremendous interest."

It was about this time I decided I wanted to be a teacher. Miss Duggan, old maid school marm, was an inspiration. And if someone could be as vivacious and fun loving as that and not be married, I'd go for it. I had seen nothing in my folks' marriage to make me want a similar life, and nothing in my dad to want to be hooked up to a man. So, I told myself with determination, *I am going to be an old maid school teacher just like Miss Duggan.*

As the years passed I joined in with the other girls jumping rope and in "red-hot-peppers", getting the initial of our husband-to-be, or throwing the long peeling of an apple over the left shoulder and looking to see what initial it foretold. I even pretended to like a certain boy so the other girls didn't think I was different, but in my heart of hearts I'd say, "No, thanks," firm in my resolve to be an old maid school teacher.

Well, Edith, if you're ever gonna amount to anything you gotta get out of the Oakie talk, 'ain't got none,' and 'where's it at?' so get set for the long pull. I believe reading will do the trick. So, read, Edith, read, I told myself.

Reading, of course, was a big help. I didn't read books, I read authors—even shelves of books, and later sections of the library. The Bible gave me a feeling for fine literature. The hymns we sang on Sunday gave me some appreciation for poetry.

In Charge of the Class

In Cotati Grammar School Miss Ball was a combination principal and sixth grade teacher. When her duties as principal called her out of the room she would pick out a good reader and hand over a book and say, "Read. I'll be back soon." She found, when coming back into the room, when Edith was reading, the kids were listening with interest. I got the job permanently.

What the kids didn't know was that Mrs. Ball had a double purpose for my reading. She had decided I was best able to keep order when she was out of the room. She also determined to teach me not to suck my thumb. Every time she saw me with my thumb in my mouth, she'd walk over with the book, and say, "Read, Edith," and go back to her desk to correct papers. Of course, I learned to ham it up to keep the attention of the kids. I also learned not to suck my thumb!

Well, to become a teacher I must get good grades, I admonished myself. So I applied myself to my studies. It wasn't all that hard. Due to Mama's action years ago, having me repeat the first grade, and due to the stupidity of school officials who thought any transfer pupil from Oklahoma should be put back a year, I was older than most of my classmates.

As I was small for my age and immature physically I fit in socially and had an easy time of schoolwork. That is, in all but spelling and music. My ears could often not distinguish sounds well and spelling was a dread. Singing was actual torture. I could tell some sounds were wrong but I didn't know whether the right sound was higher or lower.

As I grew older and fit into various organizations I'd sometimes be offered the job of secretary. "No, thanks," I'd reply quite firmly. "I can't spell." No doubt people thought I was untruthful, but so be it. I can't spell. All through my teaching career I'd set up an elaborate system of points for pupils catching me in mistakes. Often I'd pull boners on purpose, of course, but the system saved face when a spelling error came into view. And we all know what fun it is to find teacher made mistakes.

Music by Dorothea

My wonderful younger music-major soprano-singing sister Dorothea solved the music problem during my teaching years. She put all the fourth grade songs on the old Wollensak tape recorder, even using a second tape recorder to sing two part songs. When I changed grade levels she did it again for the fifth grade. And, bless her singing heart, she did it once more when I decided to teach sixth grade.

A PTA scholarship enabled me to go to college and get my teaching diploma. The year 1937 was the last year permanent teaching credentials were given and it was only due to Ray's insistence that I received my credential. Pregnant just two months after marriage ("Didn't know it was so easy," was Ray's famous innocent remark) and sick every morning, I was all for quitting college. "I promised your mother if she would give her permission for our marriage I'd see that you finished college," Ray reminded me.

Never mind that Ray lost his job and moved to Los Gatos. Never mind that I had to go back, a newly married woman, to working for my board and room. Never mind I was a victim of morning sickness. The daily streetcar ride to San Francisco State Teacher's College was torture. However, thanks to Ray's strong will and my obedience, I did finish college.

Another Teacher in the Family

Charleen arrived in our family a bare ten and a half months after our wedding. And of course, teaching was not in the picture at that time. My desire to teach was put on hold as our family grew. Glen came seventeen months after Charleen. When Charleen went to school she, not her mother, became a teacher. Daily she went over her lessons with her younger brother.

Her teaching was so well done, and Glen's learning so successful we had him go directly into first grade when he entered school. He'd already done all the kindergarten work.

My desire to teach was put on hold for a long time. I helped in Ray's various businesses, ran a boarding home for children for ten years, taught Sunday School, was a Camp Fire leader, and a counselor at Lake Hume Bible Camp.

When our youngest child, Jon, was kindergarten age and the two older ones were needing help with college expenses I decided it was time to dust off that 1937 lifetime teaching certificate.

STATE OF CALIFORNIA

To all to whom these Letters shall come, Greeting:

The Department of Education of the State of California, through the

San Francisco State College

on recommendation of the faculty of the College has conferred upon

___EDITH BROOKOVER ROBERTSON___

who has satisfactorily completed the requirements therefor, the Degree of

Bachelor of Arts

with all the rights, privileges and honors thereunto appertaining

Given by the Department of Education of the State of California, at San Francisco, this ___thirtieth___ day of ___July___ nineteen hundred ___thirty-seven.___

True Copy of Diploma for Issuance of Credential
Must not be detached

Alexander C. Roberts
President of the College

Walter F. Dexter
Director of Education and
Superintendent of Public Instruction

This is to Certify that ___EDITH BROOKOVER ROBERTSON___ has completed the full course of study and training prescribed, and has complied with the requirements fixed by the State Board of Education of California for the

General Elementary School Credential

Dated at San Francisco, California ___July 30, 19 37___

Alexander C. Roberts
President of the College

The Commission of Credentials

by authority of the

California State Board of Education

hereby issues upon the foregoing diploma and certification this

General Elementary School Credential

to ___EDITH BROOKOVER ROBERTSON___ { Void until numbered by Commission of Credentials } No. DC- 25141.

County and City and County Boards of Education are empowered, in accordance with section 5.170 of the School Code of California, to issue to the said person a General Elementary School Certificate authorizing the holder to teach any or all subjects in all grades of any elementary school in the county.

COURSE IN U. S. CONSTITUTION COMPLETED.
Countersigned by

Evelyn Clement
Assistant Secretary

Lewis P. Fletcher
President State Board of Education

Dated at Sacramento ___July 30,___ 1937.

Valid during life of holder unless revoked by California State Board of Education

Walter F. Dexter
Superintendent of Public Instruction and
Ex Officio Secretary, State Board of Education

My lifetime teaching credential, along with my college diploma. Note the inscription at bottom center; *"Valid during life of holder unless revoked by California State Board of Education."* They stopped issuing these soon after.

Teaching for Pay

In 1956 when I was 42 years old I became a real "getting-a-salary" teacher. When the kids asked me how long I'd been a teacher my reply was, "Oh, I've been dealing with kids for many, many years." And no way did I tell the other teachers it was my first year.

Twenty years of public school teaching ended mid-term when Ray became ill and needed me as caregiver. For many years I was once more a stay-at-home gal.

Church work and gardening satisfied me for some years, and then I became restless. Not enough money for lots of travel. Can't think of any hobby I'd like to pursue. What do I want to do with my remaining years? Why, teach, of course. My waning energy level wouldn't allow me to do full time work, even if some school officials would consider hiring a gal who was getting close to eighty.

Eighty Years Old and Back to Teaching

I got an appointment with Linda, the principal of Los Gatos Christian School, and told her all the marvelous things I could do for and with fourth, fifth or sixth graders. She said, "But we desperately need you in the first grade to help with our reluctant readers."

"Oh, well, teaching is teaching," I assured myself. "I can get coaching from the master teacher." The first year was delightful. I felt useful. The hours passed quickly, and when I was helping the kids I forgot all my eighty-year-old arthritic pains.

The next year I was assigned a different master teacher. I had thought Trisha a delight but Janet was outstanding in every way. I have never known anyone who so consistently applies the positive. The kids in her classes are constantly being "caught being good." I was happy being with a great teacher and twenty eager-to-learn kids.

As of this date (February, 2007), I am 92.9 years old. For six years I was a reading aide in the first grade at Los Gatos Christian School in the mornings. For two years I helped in the fourth grade. When I was eighty-eight years old I decided I no longer had the patience needed for teaching.

I do some Bible study. I host a twice-monthly Bible study and go to monthly senior meetings. I go on many short trips with the Calvary Church seniors. I read hours every day, do some light gardening, and type on my memoirs.

My three "kids" help me as I age. The Lincoln Manor retirement community had a vacancy, but I was not ready to leave this delightful garden home. Lately my granddaughter Karin and her girls have come to help. I'm learning more and more.

This seems a suitable way to spend my last years. ✍

An Athlete I'm Not

When I was a little girl in Shawnee, Oklahoma, my brother and I played with the neighbor kids hide-and-go-seek and kick-the-can. Summer evenings we collected fireflies in glass jars. Following an Oklahoma summer rain we became engineers, making elaborate dams and diverting the streams. After a winter snow we made snow balls, constructed forts, make snowmen. Our family often went to Uncle Tilt and Aunt Lottie's farm for a Sunday visit. We kids enjoyed going down into the woods with cousins Carroll and Aileen. We'd climb trees, wade in the creek, pick wild flowers. "Let's see if we can find the big turtle that lives down by the creek," we'd say, and race down through the trees. "It's my turn to ride on his back!" Once Carroll and Wilbur carved their initials on the turtle's back. Girls didn't have pocketknives.

As we grew, the boys and girls began to play different games. In the rural community of Cotati, in northern

California, the boys didn't jump rope, although they might show off their muscle by taking an end of the long jump rope, turning for us, especially if we were doing "red hot peppers." Jump rope, even if the boys disdained it, was no sissy game. We quite often jumped so long the arms of the turners would get too tired to keep turning. It was not considered remarkable for a girl to jump to the count of two or three hundred. Our recesses were ten minutes long. One day when Adelheid was first to jump she was still jumping without a miss when the recess bell rang. I wasn't that good but I wasn't too bad, either.

I lost my interest in reading the Bobbsy Twins serials when the author had one of the girls in a dramatic moment faint, because she had jumped to one hundred. Ha! How silly! Even little kids could jump to one hundred!

We girls played various games of hopscotch, drawing our elaborate patterns with a stick in the dirt, marking with our initial the "poison" square reserved for our private use.

Hopscotch was girls' game but the boys and girls joined forces when it came to marbles. For our Cotati school game of marbles we dug holes in the playground dirt in a pattern similar to that used in lawn croquet. We had elaborate rules. We "lagged" for "who goes first." For lagging we stood back of a drawn line and gave our marble an underhanded toss toward the beginning line. We got to shoot in the order of how close we were to the start line. We "spanned," or "double spanned" at certain parts of the game. For spanning, after getting a marble in a hole, we put our thumb on the edge of the hole, then made a mark in the dirt with our middle finger as a place for the next shot of our marble. Large hands were an advantage in spanning. We always paired off with boy-girl partners. It was fortunate that Cotati was a small school.

To play many games boys and girls teamed up. It was very common to have boys and girls in the seventh and eighth grade play together.

I became aware that I was not proficient as an athlete. Albert was usually my partner because he was one of the best at marbles and I was one of the worst. When we made teams for other games I was usually teamed up with a superior athlete, usually Albert or Bernardo, the tallest boys. There was no comment. No one made fun of me. It was just accepted Edith needed help to make the teams come out even.

I was in large Petaluma Junior High in the second half of the seventh grade when I went to live with Grandma. In a school that size there was no more boy-girl playing games. The gym was huge, with definite sections for boys and girls. My fellow athletes were all girls. I didn't do very well. I don't think I was ever the very last to be chosen for a team, but I was usually near the last. Girls were not expected to run long distances so the frequent practice I'd had keeping Wilbur company when he ran the two miles to Cotati in the evenings did not get any recognition. In short sprints I was one of the slower runners.

There wasn't a single sport in which I did well. In tumbling, somehow I got heavy weight Meriam landing head first right in my stomach. And no way could I stand on my head, even when the coach explained I could practice in a corner. Top of the pyramid because I was small? No, Edith would fall and mess up the formation.

Play basketball? Well, I tried. When the basketball came my way, I got my hands outstretched to catch it but ended up with a dislocated little finger.

Baseball? I never ever hit the ball. I often walked to first, however. The pitchers would take pity on me. When my team was out in the field, I was far out in center field where I would do little damage.

Volleyball? I could get the ball over the net, usually, but with an easy high looping ball that got slammed back at us. I did learn to get under a returned ball and set it up for better players.

In 1956, for my first year of teaching at Haman School in Santa Clara, how did I manage to teach physical education? Fortunately, I started in the fourth grade. Soccer was not yet popular. The kids liked to play kick ball, jump rope, hopscotch and jacks.

The schools were not into physical fitness in a big way when I first started to teach. A few years later America was getting ashamed of the poor showing our kids made compared with kids in Europe; President Kennedy was challenging us with his exercise record, "Chicken Fat." Exercises I could lead, of course. And eventually I made a trade with another fourth grade teacher, Al, a PE major, for him to take my class for PE while I took his class for English Composition or Handwriting.

The last year I taught I hired Karen, a PE major from San Jose State, to teach physical education for me while my friend Steve, the principal, chose not to know I was spending my own money. He pretended Karen was just an ordinary student teacher. Actually, the kids that year had the finest of coaching as Karen reported daily to her San Jose State coaches to get instructions.

My students in the lower grades liked me, put up with my weaknesses. One boy wrote at year-end evaluation time,

"Don't worry about being a bad umpire. You make just as many mistakes on one side as on the other side, so it is sorta fair, in a way."

An athlete I'm not, but I can sure recognize one. One afternoon on recess duty at Union School I blew my whistle and signaled Steve to come to me. "Get on over with the sixth graders where you belong," I directed.

"But I'm not a sixth grader, " he grinned. "I'm in fourth grade."

"You are a sixth grader in sports," I replied, "Now move on over where you belong." When he graduated from Leigh High School, Steve had his choice of three scholarship offers: baseball, football, and basketball.

One swimming instructor told me I'd had a lot of nerve to supervise swimmers in my back yard pool for years with no real ability to swim. I never had any trouble. I don't know how to swim well, but I do know how to supervise kids. I met a young man in Thrifty Drug Store years ago and he grinned, and asked, "Do you remember me? I'm the one who can never, ever, as long as I live, ever go swimming in your pool again." He had disobeyed my rules, sat on the edge of the pool when I'd gone to answer the phone.

I've taught kids to swim and they swim circles around me. I've taught kids to dive but I'm afraid to go off the diving board. Sidestroke is my favorite stroke. It doesn't get my hair wet.

My poor athletic ability followed me into my adult leisure life. Ray was patient with me. He tried to teach me to dance, even got Ted, with his big feet, to let me put my feet on his feet and try to learn to dance that way. We tried, but it didn't go well.

Tennis, anyone? Or badminton? Ray played with his left hand, and scored higher.

Golf? "Just keep me company, Honey," my golfing husband Ray asked. I often did keep him company. I would play just on the putting greens then tag along as he played a regular game. Our scores were about the same when we headed for home, mine for just putting and his for playing the regular course.

One time Ray made a beautiful shot off the fourth putting green. We watched the perfect arch and then saw the ball roll close to the pin. We knew it had to be near the hole. We looked closely but couldn't find the ball.

After we'd hunted for a while he said, "Oh, well, just pull the flag and I'll drop a ball and go from there." To our delight we found he'd made a hole in one. "My third hole in one!" Ray exclaimed. "But this is the only one that counts. It's the only one with a witness." I was happy to be his witness.

An athlete I'm not, but I sure can recognize one!

Control

I learned at a very early age to take care of young children. My skill came naturally as little sisters came into our family every two or three years. By the time LaVerne came in 1922 when I was eight years old, I simply presumed she was my special little girl. Mama was not well and my ability to love and care for LaVerne was appreciated. As soon as LaVerne was past the infant stage I had her with me much of the time. I had no need for dolls. I had a real live doll. The other sisters, Ruth, Lela, and Babbie just naturally came along. We were a group at play in the house, the yard and sometimes in the neighbors' yards.

When we moved from Petaluma to Cotati I was in the fourth grade. There the girls had a recess game called Ball Hopscotch. I had never heard of it in the seven schools I had attended. The Cotati Ball Hopscotch game was played with a tennis ball (or any small ball about that size). The girls took turns with the ball and counted as the one who was "It" went through a series of elaborate maneuvers while bouncing the ball. It was something like playing jacks, except we used legs and hands with the ball instead of jacks. There would be frequent arguments. "You're out." "Your leg touched the ball." "You forgot to do your 'Twosies'." "You have to do 'Round the World'." I was in the new school less than two weeks when the girls started to look to me as if I invented the game. When there was an argument the girls would look to me and I'd make the call. Somehow the air of authority had come along with me to Cotati.

Miss Ball, the sixth grade teacher and also the principal, put me in charge of the class when she was called to her office. I learned to show off a bit and be very dramatic to hold the attention of the kids. Miss Ball tried to give others a chance to be in charge, but she'd come back to noise and confusion unless I was in charge. After a while when she was called out, she'd simply nod at me and I'd walk up to the front of the class. No problem.

When I worked for my board and room from the seventh grade on through college, I depended on fun and games to manage the children left in my care. When that wasn't quite enough to get the results I wanted I'd reinforce my commands with a swat on the little one's rear end. I did not argue with the verse in Proverbs which said, "Spare the rod and spoil the child." Children are great forgivers. A few minutes after a spank I'd have a hug and smile and, "What game can we play now?"

When I became a teacher life became more difficult. I'd have forty fourth graders in one class room, some reading at first grade level and the others ranging all the way up to eighth grade level. Some were quiet, even withdrawn, and some had so many built-in wiggles they were constantly in danger of exploding. The teacher preparation classes at State College hadn't told me how to handle the combination of needs. I did the best I could. I built in variety in the lessons, planned to have the students on their feet frequently, hammed up the story hour, and gave many excuses for laughter. And then, once in awhile, I resorted to force. I used force to pull a child in line, I tapped the head of the kid who was getting a drink without permission.

The ability to control can be a handicap. I can go to a party and tell how much better the hostess could have arranged the food, how she should have used a different seating plan, why she needed to be better able to guide her guests to the front door and on out to their cars.

Once I remember the Los Gatos PTA used poor judgment in a Halloween party and the kids in the auditorium looking for fun became bored. They got noisy, and were beginning to riot. I stood up and quelled the brawl with my schoolteacher whistle, but I earned the enmity of the Los Gatos Superintendent of Schools, because he had not been able to handle the uproar. Later, when I was applying for a teaching position, his humiliation over my control of that Halloween riot was remembered and used against me.

The desire to control dies hard. It isn't a great help in a marriage. Once in a while Ray would remind me, "I'm not one of the kids, you know."

I used the control ability once to near disaster. I belonged to a Sunday School Class of seniors at Los Gatos Christian Church. I got tired of not knowing who was sitting behind me, so one Sunday I went early and pulled the chairs out of their stiff rows and made a large circle. My fourth graders had always liked being in a circle.

"There, that will be so nice. We can be more social," I said to Carol, another early arriver. She gave her purse a toss and helped me tug the chairs into the circle.

One by one the seniors trickled into the room. Some looked puzzled. Some frowned. One woman took a quick look and shouted, "I'm out of here!" She shot out the far door, heading to an upstairs class. Another said, "Well, this will be my last time in this class," as she sat down.

When the teacher came into the room I met him at the door. "We have a near riot in the senior class!" I whispered, then told him what I'd done and the reaction

'You sit tight, Edith. I'll handle it," he said. As the class settled down he announced, "We've made an experiment, but we've found we don't like it. Next Sunday we'll all be back in rows. Next Sunday back to rows. Next Sunday no more circle. Back in rows next Sunday." Since he wouldn't let me take the blame I wrote a letter to the Board of Elders telling how the teacher had handled the mess. What a super man.

Since he handled my mistake so gracefully I had no apologizing to do. A few Sundays later someone bragged about how we seniors are young at heart and just as flexible as young people. Several other seniors voiced agreement, I turned around from my seat in that rigid row and said, "Well, think that through once more. Remember when someone tried to put the chairs in a circle?"

Being a good loser was not one of my strengths.

Control – Good and Bad

When I was a little girl I was shy but I quickly developed the ability to control, at least in the home situation. Mama put me in charge of my younger sisters. I never thought whether being in control was a good idea. I just took over. No one praised me, no one criticized me. I was just boss.

As time went on I used my competency in school. I was often the recognized authority in games. I remember wondering why the other school kids looked to me to settle an argument. Sometimes, without really knowing the finer points of the game, I'd hand down my decision and it would be accepted.

What was a real strength, my capacity to control, had a flip side. I became so used to being in command I accepted responsibility for which I had absolutely no competence.

I remember being asked to lead the singing at a meeting. I have no ear for music and little understanding of musical phrases, but that didn't stop me. I took on the job. In blissful ignorance, I directed the singers, "You on this side, sing the first line, you over here, sing the alternate line." Bless their sweet little hearts. They tried.

Another time the vacation Bible School leader put me in charge of the youth rhythm band. In that instance the young redheaded pianist, with her peppy and very loud playing, saved me from utter catastrophe.

I recently started logging on daily to a one minute Neil Anderson devotional. He takes a Bible verse and makes comments about it. I find his observations helpful. He recently had some thoughts based on I Corinthians 6:12: "All things are lawful for me, but not all things are profitable".

Some of his examples:
physical rest can become laziness
ability to profit can become avarice and greed
physical pleasure can become sensuality
enjoyment of food can become gluttony
caution can become unbelief
loving-kindness can become overprotection
judgment can become criticism
anger can become rage and bad temper

Anderson didn't mention one of my great strengths, my ability to control, but I know very well what the flip side is—the negative, the weakness. It may well be a short trip but it is a trip I too often make—the move from control where control is needed, to downright bossiness.

What makes the control problem so difficult is that the ability is both good and evil. It's a sort of tightrope walk.

I've always had trouble with the control. Elder son Glen has given me tips over the years. Once he was downright determined, "Mother, what you are calling good management is manipulation. You are not always right, you know. And even when you are right, you have to learn to let go."

I'm still struggling. I know the steps to take to make changes. I need to ask God for wisdom to know what changes to make. If I study the Bible and memorize Scripture to store God's wisdom in my heart and maintain my prayer life I come out ahead in the private battle with control. Some verses that have helped me:

Hebrews 4:17	To one who knows the right thing to do and does not do it, to him it is sin.
Galatians 6:9	Let us not lose heart in doing good.
Philippians 4:13	I can do everything through Him who gives me strength.

Substitute Teaching - 1955

With Jon in kindergarten I visited various classes at old Los Gatos Grammar School on University Avenue and the new Louise Van Meter School on Los Gatos Boulevard to get a feeling for the level I'd like. Somehow I settled on fourth grade. Lucy Fay Papac influenced me. She had taught fourth grade so long she was now teaching the offspring of her first pupils and she still found the age level fun.

When I graduated from San Francisco State Teachers College in 1937 I received a permanent teaching credential. However, permanent or not, I knew I was not ready to teach. I registered at San Jose State, taking courses I felt I needed. I initialed my own course applications, ignoring the posted advice to get a counselor. My system worked well the twelve years I continued in postgraduate work at State, West Valley and California University.

I entered teaching by the back door. I put my name on the Santa Clara County substitute list, asking to be called for fourth, fifth, or sixth grades.

If I had only known! Substituting is not teaching. Substituting is just holding the fort. The sub is regarded as fair game for insubordination. The better teachers leave lesson plans but no one can tell all the details. Some ineffectual teachers leave no plans or plans impossible to follow. One unproductive lesson plan for the entire day simply said: Practice Play. I had trouble with discipline and the principal scolded me. "Just because the teacher was an idiot doesn't excuse you. You should have given a spelling test, then a math test, then had a very structured lesson in grammar." So, I learned.

Gradually I worked out the skills needed to hold a class. I developed special art lessons, spelling games and math contests. I learned to put the most popular boys in charge of the physical education period. I chose thrilling stories to read.

In the 1950's portable tape recorders were heavy, expensive and a novelty. The kids loved to listen to themselves sing or read or give book reports on the Wollensack Recorder Ray had given me. They would often have to be chased away at recess time from their self-love. If I had an especially difficult class I might mention their "real teacher" could be left a recording of their class.

My teaching experiences varied day by day. One Cambrian fifth grade watched me critically. I sensed a time bomb was ready to explode. Using one of my trick lessons early in the morning I organized a spelling baseball game. Usually I'd try to see that the "big shot" of the class would keep score as he, in turn, would keep things under control. This time I noticed a boy with a dull apathetic look and I knew, instinctively, that he could not spell, would be humiliated at the exposure, so I chose him to keep score. Immediately the class discarded the tense judgmental mood. I had passed their test. I shuddered to think how close I had been to utter ruin.

One time a phone call came for me late in the morning. In fact, it was an hour into the school day so I knew they were scraping the bottom of the substitute barrel.

"You are needed to take a kindergarten class over in Saratoga."

"But I'm not down for kindergarten. I've signed up for fourth, fifth, and sixth."

"Well, yes, we know that, but we need you for a kindergarten class."

"I've never taught kindergarten. I don't know the first thing about kindergarten."

"Please, give it a try. The principal is holding the class and we can't find anyone certificated to take it, and he has important meetings scheduled."

I was given a quick "Hello—Thanks—" at the door of the kindergarten by the principal on his way out. Then a young towhead looked up at me. "I'm William Morgan Ferguson the Third, but you can call me Bill. Anything you need to know, I'll tell you."

He was my Jon's age. I knew how smart Jon was. I relaxed. "Well, what do we do first, Bill?"

Bill proceeded to organize the class and led us, step by step, through the entire day. The kids respected his authority and I followed closely. The day went beautifully. We got through the carpentry part without a mishap as Bill's eagle eye was on each kid. I felt a bit guilty when my pay came that month. I knew who had earned that $15.00.

In one confusing sixth grade class in San Jose during the spelling period three pupils left for another class (not a thing in the lesson plans to clue me in) and in flounced three mature gum-chewing girls, taking the vacated places, legs out into the aisles, opening strange text books and pretending to work. I passed them paper, told them to take the spelling test; no one was excused. They declared they were eighth graders there for just one period. With no lesson plans to guide me, I stared them down, insisting on dominating the situation. When I reported the strange incident in the teacher's room my credibility went up. The girls had been sent down to the lower grade for discipline. My getting them to take a sixth grade spelling test was considered remarkable.

Somehow I got through the subbing experience. It was a constant challenge, more a battle than teaching. I picked up a million ideas for later use and earned enough, barely, to keep me going. I developed a sympathy for substitutes that stands to this day. Regardless of what money a sub is paid she has earned more than double her take-home wage.

During that one year, while subbing and taking courses at State College, I applied for a permanent teaching job in various districts

Once when I kept an appointment for an interview in Cupertino I was left sitting on a hard chair in a poorly lighted office for two hours. I had nothing to read. I heard no conversation in the adjoining rooms. After a half hour had passed I became concerned about the heavy commute traffic for my trip home. Another half hour passed. Eventually almost two hours passed. Jon would be home from kindergarten. I had never left him alone for long. Then the principal finally appeared. Without an apology, he shot many fast questions at me, picking up part of answers to criticize without letting me complete a sentence. Abruptly he stood. "I do not like your voice. It shows signs of strain, is not soft and well modulated. We cannot use you."

I was glad to escape from him and his idea of an interview. ✍

A Full Time Teacher - 1957

Nobelium (element 102) discovered in Stockholm. (I think we had only 92 to memorize when I was in chemistry class in 1932). International Year is proclaimed by 87 cooperating nations. Bobby Fischer, 13 years old, was chess champion. "Beat" and "Beatnik" took hold as words to describe the "Beat Generation". *The Bridge on the River Kwai* won an Academy Award. President Eisenhower sent the National Guard marching into Little Rock to enforce desegregation.

My teacher applications resulted in many interviews. Most of the interviews went well. Each time, I showed my 1937 teacher's certificate and told of my background in Camp Fire, Cub Scouts, and the boarding home for children. "I've heard of these lifetime certificates, but this is the only one I've even seen," one principal said.

I was quite a "buy" to a district. I had had twenty years of experience with kids and would start with a low-on-the-salary-scale wage.

Disadvantage to be overcome? I was older than many of the principals and might suppose I knew more. I accepted a fourth grade class in Santa Clara at Haman School, where gentle, soft-spoken Arthur Bubb was principal. He daily coped with one of his former teachers, now teaching under him. At faculty meetings we often heard her interrupt, "Now, Arthur—" as she'd try to direct him. He handled her interruptions with fond patience. He was used to older women. I didn't have to worry about my age and experience threatening him.

As soon as my contract was signed I asked for all the textbooks for the coming year. I cannot forget the surprised look on Mr. Bubb's face. The surprise was mutual. I had not thought a teacher would have the nerve to teach one day at a time, just one jump ahead of the kids. He was equally surprised to meet a teacher who had all the intentions of being well prepared.

I studied each text, made tentative plans and took more courses as I sensed my weaknesses. I was frightened of the prospect of teaching music. That summer I took courses in classroom music, rhythm instruments, and folk dancing. I bought music bells.

Helpers

My friend, Anna Pate, recorded all forty-six songs from the little green California State Text, Folk Songs of the United States, for me. Fifty years later I can still see fat, fun-loving Anna, rocking on her piano bench, as she belted out *Make My Living In Sandy Land*, then *Buffalo Gals Won't You Come Out Tonight?*, and *Old Noah He Built Himself An Ark*.

My younger sis, music major Dorothea, recorded all the songs from the fourth grade music book for me, accompanying herself on the piano. When there was a two-part song she put the first part on the tape, then while we played it on one recorder, she sang the second part to go with it. All summer, as I went about my housework, I listened to the tapes.

MEMORIES OF MY FIRST STUDENTS

Charles, part Indian, saying, "Who, me?" when someone said, "—and this Indian—." Manuel, talking about Mexican food, "It's the chili that makes it so good." Carl, ashamed of lower level books needed to improve his skill, taking the books out of the library "to read to my little sister." Jean, exceptionally bright and a top athlete, running less than her best so Charles could come in first, blushing, then looking defiant as she saw her teacher noticing what she was doing.

Linda, a top reader deliberately reading poorly, trying to be put in the afternoon reading group where there were more boys. Becky, a performer on the Mickey Mouse programs, doing her demonstrations in class and leaving the kids in awe. Redheaded Brian, going deaf, a huge hearing aid box on his desk, reaching up and turning it off when the teacher scolded the class, the other kids looking enviously and the teacher desperately holding in her laughter. The same Brian in baseball, not trusting the abilities of various basemen, getting the ground ball and speeding from base to base all by himself until he finally caught the runner at third to make the out. This time the teacher is laughing and almost crying too, as she realizes the great little guy, wanting to be in professional baseball, would never make it, since the deafness was getting more and more pronounced.

I worked hard in teaching, feeling it was my duty to try to get each kid up to grade level. I continually changed techniques, often paired off kids to get one-on-one instruction, finding that tutor and tutee both gained from the experience.

At the time I taught my first class the local Santa Clara newspaper published a section of school news. Teachers were encouraged to turn in bits of the class work. I had nerve enough to turn in some of the critiques I'd received from the kids.

STUDENT COMMENTS…

"I suggest we do not have homework to mush times—My mother thinks I learned more than any class—you was nice to me—If pospbole I will try to write a letter every day—you gave a little to mush homework—but you are doing it for our good, I guess—you went to fast on the X facts—Improve your umpire—. You teach good and you are strit and you teach spelling very good—I think you could be improved is to be a better ump in baseball—I think you could have improved in writing a little bit but I did learn not to put a loop in the d and to close the a—Have more reading and Social Studies but I don't like the homework because I am busy all through the week I baby sit with baby two months old and they are a mess at feeding time—It would be two more years before you get my brother and my dad still wishes brother gets you, because he is lazy and dose not do his work—I don't like to cretasise but Study spelling more I got a F in spelling and I tried so hard I studied at home and at school."

Supercalifragilisticexpealidocious

It was my first year of teaching. I was terrified of my new vocation. Kids I knew. But teaching was a fearful thing. How in the world was I ever going to cover all those subjects? And, most fearful of all, how would I cope with the music period? Dorothea, my musical younger sister, had encouraged me, and put all the fourth grade songs on tape for me. I played and sang with the tapes all summer until I knew them by heart.

After about six months into that first year of teaching, I was beginning to relax a bit. Then the music supervisor for Santa Clara schools came visiting one day in the teacher's lounge, asking for the best times to visit each classroom. I followed her outside when the noon recess bell rang. "I simply cannot have you observe me when I am teaching music," I pleaded. "Can't you just listen outside the window? Please, please. If I know you are taking notes, I'll freeze. I know I will."

"Tell you what, Edith. I'll do my checking in a different way. Let's go now and I'll visit your class when it is not music period. You said this next period is Social Studies? And they are working on maps?"

The kids were lined up at the door, the door monitor holding out his hand for the key. Once inside the room, lunch boxes on the shelves, baseballs and mitts thrown into the corner, the kids went to work on their California paper maché maps. Mrs. Howell strolled about the room talking briefly to some of the kids.

Arthur Bubb, my principal, grinned when he told me the music supervisor's comments. She told him of the visit, said the kids loved their teacher. One pupil had shown her the Wollensak tape recorder with the tapes of Dorothea's singing. Another had shown her the bells and rhythm instruments and still another explained how they took turns playing the autoharp and xylophone. Her comment to him had been: "It's a classic case of over-compensation. That gal has enough equipment to stock a music store."

Dorothea Taught Music for Me

So I made it through the first year. Dorothea actually taught my music period, year after year, through those wonderful tapes. It was like having her in my class. For the two-part songs she had recorded one part then played that tape on one recorder while recording again while she sang the second part. At one point she called my son Glen in from the swimming pool, and had him join in, dripping wet, to sing baritone.

The Recorder

Then, in 1971, when I was in my fifteenth year of teaching, California mandated that fourth grade kids were to learn how to play the recorder. I shuddered. I remembered when, as a seventeen-year-old high school girl, I worked at Elizabeth Jorgensen's and she tried to teach me to play the piano. I learned that the spaces spelled **F-A-C-E** and the lines said E*very Good Boy Does Fine*, but, practice as I would, I never got past the Key of C and *Wake up, Little Daisies*. If Elizabeth hadn't had the patience of a saint, she'd have given up on me completely.

I thought back to that horrible college class in Elementary School Music where I'd have flunked out except for Leona's help. The instructor had given me a courtesy C and commented, "You can carry a tune, Edith, in a bucket. I suggest you do not teach in the lower grades where music is so important."

Now, heaven help me, I was supposed to teach a wind instrument, a simplified flute called the recorder. Union School District had Larry Sampson, the music supervisor, give a series of lessons for all fourth grade teachers. Some went in protest, not needing Larry's guidance, but I went eagerly. No one was more faithful. No one handled that twelve-inch plastic instrument with greater determination. No one paid greater attention. Larry took us, step-by-step, through the various fingerings. After a few lessons with Larry the little black junior flutes arrived for the kids and it was the teachers' turn to put what we had learned into practice.

Each week I went to Larry's lessons for the teachers and each week I taught the kids what I had learned. The lessons went well. The kids loved their recorders. Coming from poor families, most had never had their hands on a music instrument. They gave great care to their recorders, often took them home to practice. The kids waited impatiently for their turn to play my large wooden tenor recorder or the brass baritone. Soon we had to reserve an area outside the classroom where those who wanted to practice during recess would be away from flying balls and running kids.

The ten-year-olds became used to their recorders. The novelty wore off but their love lasted. Sometimes I'd see a few kids playing in tune as they marched home. They packed their recorders when they went on trips.

Marty, the Super Player

Our top player was show-off Marty. Each time I presented a lesson he was smugly confident. He'd already figured out how to do it. I went to Larry in despair, "Larry, what am I supposed to do with a kid who knows it all? He's 'way beyond my help. He's getting notes out of that recorder that we haven't come to yet in our lessons—notes I don't know how to do."

"Leave him alone, Edith. He's a natural. He's compensating with his mouth for the fingering he still doesn't know. Don't hamper him in any way."

The principal asked our class to perform for Home and School Club. We worked out a program of the kids' favorites. Marty said, "I'll do *Supercalifragilisticexpialidocious* (a song made popular by the 1964 Disney movie *Mary Poppins*) for a solo number. See how I can play it," and, without waiting for a reply, he had his recorder at his mouth and was ripping out the melody.

"Yeah, let him do it!" the kids begged. "We know he can do it okay. It's got so many ups and downs. It's not easy to play. People will be surprised."

I gave in to them and we put Marty on as the last person on the program. "And what do you plan to do if you make a mistake?" I asked.

"I won't make a mistake."

"Yes, I hear you. But if you make a mistake, what will you do?"

"I won't make a mistake."

"Let me clue you in. Even great musicians make mistakes. We will practice what you will do if you goof. I want you to play part-way through, make a mistake on purpose, then show us what you will do."

So Marty played a few measures, hit a blue note, stopped, looked at his supposed audience and said, "Excuse me."

"That's fine, Marty. It would be even better if you bowed, grinned, and then give your speech." The kids liked that idea and I kept Marty practicing for a while.

Came the night of the Home and School Club program. Our class had the last part of the program. Marty had the last number. His confidence was inspiring as he stepped forward. His fingers flew and out came the complicated rhythm. Then it happened. A blue note. Marty held his recorder out before him, stared at it in a puzzled way, shrugged, grinned, and said, "I wonder how that happened." He took a small step forward, gave that deep courtly bow he'd practiced for me, started at the beginning and played flawlessly.

As the fond parents clapped I thought, "You're no musician, Edith, but you are a teacher." ✍

Fourth Grader Jerry

I have had many loves and a few short-term hates in my life. They range from my early childhood to my present old age. A very great number of loves were developed over my twenty years of teaching. I'll mention the hates first because there weren't many of them and they didn't last long. I find it impossible to hate anyone after I get to know him. I think it was Lincoln who said, "I never knew any man I could hate very long."

I used to give swimming parties during the summer for my coming fourth graders. The mothers and I would get acquainted while the kids had a good time in the pool. One time as I sat by Mrs. Mirassou her son Jerry threw a tennis ball fiercely at the near wall and perilously close to his mother's head. The ball bounced back to Jerry and he repeated the throwing. "He's upset because I said we'd come to get acquainted but with his cold he couldn't go in the pool," Mrs. Mirassou explained.

I nodded but to myself I said, "There's one kid I'm going to have to pray over to get to liking. What a brat! Why doesn't his mother make him get a bit further away with his ball throwing?"

After getting acquainted with Jerry I realized his mother was calm because she knew her boy's athletic ability. He had perfect control over that ball. I saw him in baseball season brushing back the batter just like the big league pitchers. And, of course, I didn't have to do any praying to get to love Jerry. He was very bright, always ready with an original remark, a natural leader. At the first parent conference his mother took his report card, glanced at it and said, "I'm going to have to ask you to take these A's and change them to B's. Jerry works best with a challenge." I let her have her way but I did not make the corresponding changes on the duplicate report card in the cum folder.

Jerry was the second son of the Mirassou Winery owners. He often came to school in patched jeans. That was in the days when only poor people wore patches. Ann Mirassou, knowing her boys would be wealthy, was determined to help her boys appreciate the real world. Jerry earned his spending money by daily cleaning out the rest rooms of the Mexican winery workers. Besides learning to work hard, he picked up Spanish.

Once he brought me a bottle of Mirassou wine. When I told him I didn't drink wine he took back the bottle of wine and brought me a bottle of grape juice. Woody, the principal, told me I'd certainly made a poor exchange.

Jerry and I became great friends. He was what I call a "Sparkler." His comments often were a bit wild but they added fun to the lessons. Once he got a bit too carried away and made a smarty remark about my teaching. I turned on him, "If you think it is so much fun to teach that you could do it better, I'll let you try your hand at it. You take Joey outside and don't come in again until you've taught him three useful facts."

Joey was a brain-damaged boy lodged in my class for a few days until the school officials could complete the paper work to get him in a special class. Jerry looked at me to see if I was serious, and saw my anger.

He grabbed some pencils and paper then took Joey by the hand. "Come on, Joe," he said, and out they walked. I glanced out the window later and saw both boys sitting next to a basket ball standard, heads close together. As time passed I kept looking out the window. Once I saw them walking about. Once they were shooting baskets. And for a time they disappeared.

A long time later the two boys came into the classroom. "Show the teacher," Jerry instructed and Joey shyly walked to the front of the room and proudly handed me a sheet of paper with his first and last name in block letters.

"He already knew how to write his first name," explained Jerry to me. Then he nudged Joey. "Now show her the next paper."

Joey showed the next sheet with his address on it. "We went to the office and found where he lives," he told me.

"Now show the next paper," Jerry instructed. The third sheet of paper had Joey's phone number. "And I can read them by myself," said Joey as Jerry directed him to his seat.

Joey gave me a look of pride and satisfaction, and then went to his seat. Jerry also went to his seat and also gave me a look of pride and satisfaction but it was mixed with a sassy, "Ha! Ha! I beat you on that one!"

Reading for Recreation

I don't remember learning to read. The first grade teacher, burdened with forty kids, in her first year of teaching, wrote glowing compliments for each pupil, but Mama over-rode the teacher and had me repeat the first grade. She explained later, "Honey, you couldn't count past ten and barely knew your colors. I don't think you could say the alphabet, much less read."

WITHOUT PHONICS

It must have been in that second year of first grade that things began to fall into place. Suddenly, I knew how to read. I was a *look-and-say* reader. I didn't learn phonics until I had to teach phonics to my fourth grade classes. Today I refuse to get overly enthusiastic about phonics. I learned without phonics and I confess I'm a bang-up reader.

I've been reading in all my extra time ever since the second grade. Once, on a trip to the big brick Shawnee,

Oklahoma, library I rushed to the kids' corner. I tugged a book forward. "I've read this one. No, not this one. This one is too hard. Oh, here's a new Mother Westwood story." I waited with Mama before the librarian's tall desk, reached up and handed the lady my book to be checked.

Years later in California I asked Mama, "Do you remember the library in Shawnee? Why did the librarian have such a high desk? My neck used to hurt, looking so far up at her."

Mama laughed, "She had an ordinary desk, Honey. You were just such a tiny girl to be checking out books. The librarian had to look down at her little customer."

LIVING THROUGH OTHERS

Once I learned to read I was set for life. What a fascinating way to explore the world, to discover how other people lived. I wept and laughed with *The Little Women.* I giggled yet admired *Cheaper by the Dozen.* I honored *The Man Called Peter.* I had a lump in my throat with *Little Boy Lost.* I floated down the Mississippi River with Huck and Jim. People called it fiction but it was reality to me.

We never had money to buy books but our trips to the library were as routine as our trips to school or church. Mama read in all her spare time and one by one, all the girls of the family became avid readers. At any visit to a library we always checked out as many books as the rules allowed. We'd read all we had chosen, borrow from each other, and then re-read if we couldn't get to the library soon.

When Ray and I were married I encountered another kind of reader. As a very young reader he developed determination when he read *The Little Train Who Could.* That litany: "I think I can, I think I can, I think I can" became his life motto. When he was a kid he read, as any boy would, the classics such as *Tom Sawyer* and *David Copperfield*. Then he was fascinated by history. He read about the Mohawks and Captain John Smith. One Christmas his dad got Ray a twenty-four-volume set of Books of Knowledge. He went through the entire set, A to Z. One year he read several hundred books, then he left fiction behind and concentrated on facts.

We both loved to read but our tastes were certainly different. When I was busy reading novels Ray was reading Time Magazine or books to increase his business ability. I tried to plow through some of his textbooks on accounting and business practices. Ugh! How dull. Ray was equally bewildered by the way the kids and I all read fiction.

He'd see me with my head buried in a novel and smile in fond amusement. He'd weaned himself from fiction when he was in his early teens. Fiction was for kids.

Frequently, in a conversation, I'd make some comment which would astonish Ray. He'd ask, "Where did you learn that?" I'd take pleasure in responding, "Learned it reading a silly novel."

All three of our kids became avid readers. Their tastes range from science fiction, gothic horror, hard science, and cosmetology, to quantum electrodynamics. We frequent the library. Those with money haunt the local bookstores. I, offspring of depression, enjoy the Los Gatos Happy Dragon thrift store where books are from fifty cents to two dollars. Once in a while, when I'm browsing, I see a sign "**Books 50% Off Today.** " Oh, joy! I grab a shopping cart and load up. Books to read and books to share.

Our well-heeled number-one son regularly buys books and then shares with the rest of us poor folks.

Sometimes I note a newly purchased book lying on a table and my sons will hasten to say, "No, you wouldn't like this one, Mother." Then I know it is either too explicit in sexual content or it is poo-pooing my Christian beliefs. At present our favorite authors are P.G. Wodehouse, Dick Francis, and Frances Hodgson Burnett.

When and Where

Where do I read? Any place, any time. Under the covers with a flashlight when I was a kid after hearing Daddy yell, "Get that light out, you're wasting electricity!" In high school in study hall when I'd completed all my assignments. On the school bus when I didn't get to sit with a special friend. In my room when I lived with Grandma. Shivering in the cold on the outside porch when I lived with the Jorgensens. For four years on the San Francisco streetcars on my way to State College.

During early years of marriage I read when sitting up with a sick child. I sometimes stole time from sleep to read. I read as I cooked. I read as I walk. I keep a book in the car and read in heavy bumper-to-bumper traffic. If I get too engrossed in my book there's always some kind motorist who will give me a toot on his horn.

Some household chores can be done with a book in one hand. It doesn't take concentration to stir chocolate pudding. Many of my books have little flecks on them that I know came from the kitchen.

One morning I didn't hear the doorbell ring when my missionary friend from Brazil came calling. Barbara strolled in the open sliding back door, gave me a kiss and said, "Edith, I've traveled to many countries and seen some bizarre sights but this is the strangest thing I've even seen: you, vacuuming, with a book in your hand." ✍

Teaching at Lone Hill School

The United States grew again when Alaska became our 49th state on July 6, 1958—relegating Texas to *second* largest. The Soviets launched the 3,000-pound Sputnik III in October, 1957, and we responded with the 31-pound Explorer I three months later.

In September daughter Sheri went to Westmont College in Santa Barbara, got a job for $1.25 an hour at a medical lab. She wrote she liked her job and liked Westmont.

Glen had a farewell party at Ferguson's and 35-40 people came to the airport to bid him farewell. He wrote: "The Y is plush, Chicago is horrible, Moody is wonderful." His Great Aunt Elsie mothered him when he became homesick but enthusiastic letters showed he was too busy for introspection or homesickness.

Jon started second grade with only one kid he'd known from his previous class. Louise Van Meter School had taken the top kids from three previous grades and put them all in one accelerated class. Jon had been the "best" in his previous class, now he was just one ordinary kid. His teacher was pregnant, and had a sick husband. Jon came home several times and said his teacher fell asleep again in class. There were many substitutes and the principal often came in to help. It was a wasted year. Jon would have been better off at home. He missed Sheri and Glen and spent a lot of his time with Grandpa and Grandma Robertson in their house trailer in the backyard. Unbeknownst to me, Jon started experimenting with electricity and chemistry.

We saw my sister-in-law Louise, her husband Sheldon, and my neice Gloria often. Gloria rallied around to fill the gap of "no-teen-agers-here-now" that we felt keenly, and helped Ray on Saturdays at the business. Ray had some big days. September 18th he sold over $1,000 worth of typewriters—five Olympias and two Smith-Corona portable electrics.

That summer of '58, I was back at San Jose State College, this time to take a class in teaching penmanship. Three huge men slouched against the wall in the back of the class. They were each as big as Woody Linn, but no way as courteous. They paid no attention to the instructor, and maintained a constant low conversation. Obviously, all they wanted from that class was an easy unit on the salary scale. I was frustrated; I needed the information being taught. How I yearned to tell them what I thought of their boorish behavior! Why didn't they get out on to the football field where they belonged and kick a ball around?

One day after class the instructor followed me into the hall. "They are too big to fight, dear, but I will have the last word. They will get slips of paper in the mail which say they have failed the class."

School started for me at Lone Hill with pre-school meetings, my classroom to get ready, supplies to order and the usual hated bulletin boards to decorate. On September 14th the enrollment was 44, but some pupils were transferred, leaving me with "only" 41.

Early in that year of my teaching I had to cope with a boy who was already his mother's boss. Craig was so sensitive his mother told me he had to have gas for every simple dentist examination. I failed to note any sensitivity in the kid. He was a rough husky boy and had been a terror in the neighborhood and in every class from kindergarten through his two years in the third grade. In my fourth grade class that overgrown kid continued to be a bully on the playground and in the schoolroom. I tried reasoning. I tried rewards. I tried punishments.

Finally, with that huge class of 41 needing my attention, I decided to play my percentage game: one kid and his needs against the other kids and the teacher. Craig's reign of terror was about to end. A day later big Craig stomped into class after recess behind delicate little Cindy. Just inside the door Cindy bent to pick up her sweater. Frail little girl. All bent over. Defenseless. Craig swung back his hefty right foot and aimed. It was a real kidney blow, so hard that Cindy, white with pain, sprawled on the floor.

Without hesitation, I laid our big bully out flat beside Cindy. I don't remember how I did it. He was almost as big as me. But down he went. After the school nurse attended to Cindy, I turned to Craig. "I'm telling you right now, Craig, that you'll get the same thing again every time you try to pull a stunt like that."

One entire year Craig behaved in school. The next year he was back to his former actions. By the eighth grade he was so bad the frantic principal and counselors met to study Craig's cumulative folder, trying to get a clue to his actions.

The cum folder contains all the previous grades, teacher reports, incidences of misbehavior, and any items thought necessary to help teachers understand the child. The desperate counselors found that for one year, as a fourth grader, Craig had given no trouble.

The school district hired a half-day sub for me so I could meet with the psychologists and give them my "secrets." When I told them their bratty boy had behaved due to fear of me they demurred, tried to get me to admit to some other logical reason.

They didn't want to hear it but I told them anyway. "There was nothing magic about it. He walked 'the straight and narrow' that year because he was afraid of me." The last I heard of him, he was a dropout in reform school for repeatedly throwing beer bottles at people. His mother was grieving because no one understood her sensitive son.

As soon as I realized Jon's year in the second grade was a total loss I started reading and spelling lessons at home. A Mr. Dolch had made a study and found 220 words comprise 80% of a beginning reader's sight vocabulary. I made Dolch word games and drills for Jon. We continued all summer with the Dolch words and with oral reading and Jon made two years reading growth.*

Jon went regularly to Stockade meetings at the church and was several times Honor Stockader. Once when I picked him up after a meeting, he brushed off my kiss as usual and exclaimed, "I had the neatest hiding place of all the guys—right in the middle of some poison oak. No one thought of looking there." (And I got a very bad case of poison oak .)

Various relatives and friends visited from time to time. One night Jon and Cousin David, sleeping out in the little house, set a booby trap for my sister Dorothea and me.

However, we missed our usual nightly check-up visit. Both boys got drenched the next morning as they opened their door to come up to the main house.

Jon continued his interest with motors, electricity, liked to take things apart to see how they worked. He got to be such a pest, not always able to put things back together again, that I went to the district psychologist for help. "I know you are here to help us with the Union School District kids but I need help with my kid. He's driving me crazy, always taking things apart. Can you advise me?"

I was told to rejoice. Taking things apart was the beginning part of the creative process. The putting things together would follow. Well, he puts my books together now and gets me published, so it all came out ok. ✎

Jon's Note: That summer was very difficult. It started out ok; I had about a week to play and fool around outside as usual before Edith sat me down one day and told me that I would have to read an hour each day, all summer. All *summer?* All summer. I remember her words to this day: "I will *not* have an *illiterate* in this *family.*"

I still remember the tears and frustration of "Losing My Whole Summer!" But Edith was no dummy; she started me with adventure books. As the story goes, I was instructed that it wasn't *her* job to keep tabs on little boys learning to *read*, and that it was *my* job to make sure she could hear me, no matter where she was or what she was doing. So I had to follow her around the house, reading out loud for one horrible hour each and every day of that endless, torturous summer.

Edith told me years later what actually happened. One day she didn't hear me reading when I was supposed to be, and came into the living room with hard thoughts, ready to reprimand me. What she saw was a very absorbed little boy reading on the couch, totally lost in his book, moving his lips as he lived the adventures of Captain Horatio Hornblower. She quietly backed out of the room. I've been a reader ever since.

Jack LaLanne and I

At Lone Hill School we fifth grade teachers had planned our physical education program meticulously. Al Oliver took all the boys for P. E. Myrtle Sutherland took all the girls, and I took over the preliminary exercise period for all three classes. When I was about forty-four years old I was in charge of over 100 fifth graders for a fifteen to twenty minute daily exercise period.

It was the time when our pampered sedentary United States kids were being compared, most unfavorably, with the skating, walking, bicycle-riding European kids. The newspapers ridiculed our weaklings. When a song writer of the day lampooned our poor physical showing, President Kennedy challenged him to compose a helpful exercise song. Then Kennedy distributed the resulting jazzy record, *Chicken Fat*, to the every school in the United States. Since I was the exercise leader at our school, the principal put me in charge of the record.

Every day we had all 100 fifth graders race to take their places in line on the blacktop to start their P.E. period. I had several popular athletic boys and girls up front with me to help demonstrate good form. Assistants ran the record player. Helpers with class lists on clipboards took turns behind the lines, checking off names of kids from their class who were doing exceptionally well.

I used the Canadian Nurse exercise record for a warm-up, then I switched to the lively seven-minute "Chicken Fat" record. I wish I had that record today. It provided sound advice, many chuckles and very lively musical lyrics, all ending with the loud refrain, "Go, You Chicken Fat, Go."

Once in a while I had to remind some poorly motivated kid that I understood his feelings, because, after all, I was forty-four years old and I knew it was sorta hard.

Woody Lynn, my principal, complimented me on the exercise program and said he might get the San Jose Mercury News to check it out some day. How would I like to be featured in the news? Not at all, thank you. But that didn't stop Woody.

One sunny day, about half-way into the exercises, two huge television cameras rolled into place, one behind the lines of kids, the other at the side. They started cranking away at me and then at the kids.

"Oh, you Woody Lynn," I thought, and I pretended I did not see the cameras. "I'll get even with you later, Woody." The fifth graders were startled but I indicated for them to continue exercising.

Then, striding toward me, was a serious-faced Jack LaLanne and several assistants. As he approached me he peeled off his beautiful thick nubby silk robe and gravely handed it to an attendant. Then he stood, in skimpy silk blue shorts, up in front of my hundred fifth graders, and right beside me. He posed briefly, face extremely serious, holding his arms in such a position that the rolling cameras could get an excellent picture of his bulging muscles. His serious look told the kids he considered exercise very important business.

He caught the rhythm of the Chicken Fat record and joined in the exercises. Joined in? No, he led the exercises. I kept going for a short time, breathless, then walked to the back of the kids, relieved to get out of range of the cameras.

Jack LaLanne exercised up front, deadly serious, until the record came to a stop. Then, still serious, he led the kids in a few more difficult exercises, nodded, and turned to talk to Woody. The kids gave their usual joyous yells of relief and ran to the baseball diamonds.

The next morning when I came to school I found a huge silver star covering my classroom door and a sign: *Edith Robertson, Famous Television Star*.

"What is this all about?" I demanded.

"Oh, didn't you watch the television news last night? You were featured, right up front and next to Jack LaLanne."

In the September 24, 2004 issue of the San Francisco Chronicle LaLanne was featured in honor of his 90th birthday. The review stated he had started the fitness craze in America. He went from being a pimply, sickly boy to a healthy robust teenager, then fitness icon for the world. He eats 10 raw vegetables a day, takes 50 vitamins and herbal supplements. He claims to have invented many of the exercise machines in use in gyms today. He was on television for years. Many of us "old timers" remember his publicity stunts. He once did 1,000 push-ups in 19 1/2 minutes. At age 40 he towed a 2,000 pound cabin cruiser as he swam the Golden Gate Channel. At 70 he swam a portion of the Long Beach harbor towing 70 people in 70 boats. He does an hour-and-a-half weight lifting to start each day. He claims if we work at living and believe in excelling we can live a wholesome satisfying life, maybe reach 100. One of his themes is "Use it or lose it."

Jack LaLanne is six months younger than I am, but I have always known that youngsters can give sound advice to us older people. I plan to try a few of his suggestions. ✍

Union of Union

I taught for nineteen years in Union School District. Jon attended Lone Hill School for the third and fourth grades when I was teaching there.

Great grandchildren Brittany and Amanda were fifth graders many years later at Noddin School, also in the Union School district. My friend, Karen Mullaly, once a mere student teacher next to my room at Vineland School, was the capable principal at Noddin and worked herself up into the district office.

There were not many people living in Santa Clara Valley back in the 1800's. Some members of the ill-fated Donner Party settled in the area. Many of their graves can be visited at the San Jose Cemetery. Some place names, such as Shallenbarger Road, remind us of their former presence here.

People discovered the perfect growing conditions for farming and gradually farmhouses dotted the valley. The

New Almaden Mines were in production of quicksilver out at the end of what is now Almaden Avenue. There were hundred of miners. Some married miners and their families had homes scattered in the valley. The harvesting of the cinnabar ore was an ongoing activity. The cinnabar was valuable because it was used in the processing of gold. The gold was sent to the North to help finance the war. Many historians claim it was the cinnabar and the processing of gold that kept the North going successfully against the South during the Civil War.

But even though the war was going on, fathers and mothers wanted schooling for their children. That was going to be a difficult problem. People lived many miles apart. The area, sparsely inhabited, stretched from present day Campbell to the New Almaden Mines. Where were they to build the schoolhouse? It would be hours of travel for the children at the far edge of the school district.

Finally there was a solution: build the school on skids. Hitch it up to a team of horses and move it in the middle of the school year. With farms so far apart all the kids came to school by horseback. Half the time some of the pupils would have to ride horseback for many miles to get to school. Then in the middle of the school year, the others who had lived close and had a short ride, would have to ride horseback many miles.

So the school, hitched to a team of horses, moved from area to area, depending on the population of school children. The school was called Union School because the people were Union sympathizers. More people moved into the Campbell area and a school was started there. Then a school was started at the New Almaden Mine. Now Union School could have a more central location.

An elderly woman said she'd donate several acres of her farmland for the school grounds if they would agree to her rules. She stipulated:

You must have a hog-tight fence around the school grounds.
You must dig a good well for the children near the school.
You must have separate privies for the boys and girls.
If you fail in any of these provisions the land reverts to the town of San Jose.

It was a valuable gift of land, and the school officials were only too happy to sign the legal document. Over the years the population increased. Farms were subdivided, roads developed. The little country road where the school sat was called Union Avenue, for Union School. More people moved into the area with more children. It was time to build a bigger school.

"We've got to move away from this busy corner with so much traffic. And the new school will need a larger play ground," the school board members said.

"That will be easy. There are many unused acres in our old lady's grant."

"Let's tear down the old school, use the space for a school business office. We can then build a new larger school down the little side road, the Los Gatos-Almaden Road."

Lawyers researched the document. *"Separate privies for boys and girls."* Of course. *"Have a well, with good drinking water."* The courts had settled that in the past. San Jose Water Company provides good water. *"Hog tight fence around the entire grounds."* Obviously impossible. San Jose officials looked covetously at the valuable land that would be theirs if the Union School couldn't somehow find a way to break the agreement.

But, of course, any document a lawyer can put together can be dismembered by other lawyers. In a few years officials broke ground for the larger school.

Some years later, that school had to be torn down and replaced with a still larger Union School.

When the population continued to grow another school was needed. It was named Carlton School but it belonged to the same district. Then came Alta Vista School. And then another. And another. And another. Seventeen in all. They were all in the same Union School District.

So we have The Union of Union. ✍

Teaching Outside the Rulebook

Every teacher has a handful of special ways of doing things. I often watched as I saw other teachers working miracles. My son Jon, however, thinks my teaching techniques were a bit unusual. Every teacher shows educational movies, and so did I. But I had the kids taking notes as they watched. That was a bit different. Yes, I taught penmanship. I also gave every kid a piece of cardboard with a small hole punched in it. They were to cover an entire word except for one letter to test if they wrote legibly. "If you can't read that one letter without the rest of the word, your penmanship is not good." Husband Ray was indulgent, helped me buy whatever I needed for my teaching. I bought a twelve-inch plastic penmanship ruler for each kid. The ruler showed each letter of the alphabet in caps and lower case, and had sections for testing slant, legibility, and size. I liked modifying well-known *"Teacher Tricks of the Trade."*

I considered each pupil an assistant teacher. They took turns keeping track of the time spent on each subject. The time keeper of the day would stand up to signal it was time to change to the next subject in one minute. I appointed helpers in other ways, too. I had a tendency to raise my voice when I was excited or when I was scolding. That was a family trait and I thought it came from trying to be heard in a family of nine people. I'd been told my voice was not gentle and well modulated, so I was working to correct that. My helper of the day would drop a book as a signal for me to "cool it." They took delight in slamming a heavy book down with great force when I failed to lower my voice.

How We Are Put Together

I team-taught for one year in cafeteria (which also doubled as an auditorium), because we just didn't have enough classrooms at the time. There were some disadvantages to teaching in the cafeteria. There was so much space we teachers had to walk miles every day to go up and down to help individual kids. I'd hurry home after school and head for the backyard swimming pool to kick off my shoes and dunk my tired feet into the cooling water. And it was not much fun to have workers in the back kitchen. They tried hard to work quietly and they kept their voices to a low murmur, but we could occasionally hear pans drop or a mixer whir or a spoon scrape. And when the delicious cooking odors began to permeate our space, we'd all feel our noses twitch in anticipation of the coming meal. At mealtime our desks had to be in order. Anything that might tempt itchy fingers of kids coming in for lunch had to be shoved far back out of sight in each desk.

But there were many advantages. We had room to spread out the desks, to regroup them as needed or to isolate an unruly kid. And, wonder of wonders, before the noon meal and after the cleanup was completed, the kitchen was ours to use. We could send kids back to the kitchen to arrange their exhibits. The sink and counter space was sheer luxury.

In the middle of a health lesson on how food is digested I told the kids, "If we had a rabbit, skinned, I could take you all back to the sinks and show you how the insides look, how the intestines are all twined about and how the liver and heart look."

"We don't raise rabbits," Jimmy said, "but we raise chickens. I could bring one for you to show."

"Next best thing," I replied, and the following noon Jim got some attention as he cut through the broken fence of the back Vineland School playground after lunch, plucked chicken swinging casually from his hand. He was a farmer's kid; a dead chicken was no big deal to him. With the chicken was a note from Jim's dad, "I left a few feathers on for the kids to see. Happy dissecting."

The kids crammed into the cafeteria kitchen, some standing, some perched on counters behind, some crouched down so others could see over their heads but all eagerly watching as I had the fun of showing the kids what I had done a hundred times when I was a girl on our Cotati chicken ranch. I cut slowly, talking and holding up parts as I cut. I was very circumspect, and did not reveal the little inside parts that showed that this had been a rooster, not a hen. I did, however, tell them, "If this had been a hen, not a rooster, it would have had many tiny eggs of different sizes, some almost the size of a pin head and some a little bit bigger and then gradually there would've have been an egg just about ready for the hen to lay." I showed the intertwined intestines, and pulled them apart and had them guess how long they would be if not all twisted. We looked at the heart and discussed how it worked. I showed the liver and talked about its function.

I showed the gall bladder and told why we had to be very careful as we cut it off the liver. I explained how we got the expression "bitter as gall."

The lesson went well. Compliments came from parents. And, par for the course, some criticism. Woody Linn, the principal, met me after school. "I have never received so many phone calls in one day. I had to go blind and pretend I knew all about it. Next time, why don't you get my okay before you get so creative? We should have had written permission from parents."

"Good grief!" I said. "It never occurred to me to get an okay on something so commonplace as cutting up a chicken."

Teaching History

When I taught history I tried to show the passage of years by lining up students to represent different generations. We'd have a person, his child, and then that person's child. As the kids lined up they saw the time from the early Pilgrims to the Revolutionary War. Never mind that the kids on the playground later grinned and said, "Hello, Papa" and "Hi, Grandma" to each other.

We took a trip to Oak Hill Cemetery in San Jose. We walked about in the older section and read the inscriptions on the gravestones. Some dates went back many years. We gathered around Jeanette, the other fourth grade teacher, and listened to her tell of early pioneers who came to California before the gold rush days. We read the name Schallenberger (now the name of a street in San Jose) on one gravestone and heard the story of the young man who volunteered to stay alone all winter in a mountain cabin to guard the supplies while the other pioneers pushed on over the Tahoe Pass to try to get help. We learned he had very little food and only two books, the Bible and a book on good society manners.

We shivered as we heard how he listened to the wolves howl night after night and how he survived the winter of his lonely exile. When he ran out of food he'd shoot a wolf, dress the meat, nail the hide up on the outside of the cabin and cook the meat. He referred to his book, set the table correctly, and practiced formal manners very carefully as he ate. All his practice proved very helpful after his rescue when he married the daughter of the first mayor of San Jose and took his place in high society.

I had mothers helping me when we panned for gold outside the classroom. We had buckets of water to represent the river and I brought Ray's real gold pans he'd bought in the restored historic gold rush town of Columbia. The kids got sloppy wet but they had fun. Peggy's mother gave me a little glass vial of real gold particles to show the kids. "It's from Mexico, but gold is gold. Right?" Ray bought me a glass jar of fool's gold to show the kids. We visited the museum at the New Almaden Mine (the "old" or original Almaden Mine is in Spain), and learned how cinnabar ore produces mercury, which was used to separate the gold from gold-bearing ore in California. Because the mines were owned by northern sympathizers and helped provision the Union troops, that gold helped win the Civil War.

I tied in language arts with history and had the kids pretend to be pioneers and write a letter to friends back east. When one boy wrote of stopping in for a drink at Bidwell's Bar, I knew I had some re-teaching to do. A bar, in gold rush days, was a deep place in a river where loose gold collected. John Bidwell was the early settler who discovered gold before 1889 near Sutter's Fort, which later became the city, Sacramento. Oh, how often I had to remind myself: *"If they ain't learned it I ain't taught it."*

Writing Our Own History Books

I had Ray purchase composition books for each pupil. They were the standard composition notebooks with lined pages. The school district furnished spiral-bound notebooks but I didn't want those. Their pages became torn easily. In fact, the kids in the lower grades used to write on a page and tear the page out. I wanted something that seemed to cry out, "Valuable, To Be Saved." I wanted the kind I used as my diaries, the kind that would take a lot of handling and still be readable years later. *(Note: You can take a glance at the cover of this book to see the kind of notebook I'm speaking of. Look at the second line of books and especially the one with the speckled cover in the middle, right under the chain of the stopwatch; this was the type we actually used in my classroom.)* I still treasure notebooks I wrote in years ago. I have many of them stuck away on a lower shelf in my office. I pick up diary number nineteen and read what I thought was important in my life from November 2, 1935 to February 12, 1936, when I was a freshman at San Francisco State College. "That's history, Mother," Jon says. "You have to save those notebooks. They have when I got the mumps, when Glen left for college—everything!" I wanted that experience for these kids. I wanted them to be able to look back and say, "That's how it was when I was in the fourth grade at Vineland School on Almaden Avenue, San Jose." (I have willed my twenty-four remaining diaries to son Jon.)

At least three days a week, as part of the language lesson, I would signal the timekeeper of the day to get the stopwatch ready. Then I'd direct the class, "Everyone, notebooks out. Open to your last writing. Skip two lines. Put down the date and stand up." It is amazing how some kids are already standing, almost as soon as I get the words out. Slow pokes finally follow directions and stand. I continue, "Everyone ready? Sit down. Pencil in hand. Close your eyes." Of course I have to wait again for slow pokes. I look around the room to see if eyes are closed.

"Think. What did you do the last fifteen minutes? Who were you with? Where were you? What could you smell? What could you hear? How did you feel? Now put your pencil to the paper. Write!" In three minutes the timekeeper would call, "Time!"

Then I would direct, "With your pencil pointing at the last word you wrote, count backward. Put down the number of words you wrote. Tell you neighbor how many words you wrote. Now, divide by three. Put down the words per minute and tell your neighbors."

Sometimes I'd have them pick out one sentence they wanted to share with a neighbor. Sometimes we listened to volunteers read what they had written. I knew some of the volunteer readers were adlibbing, pretending they had written more but I never called their bluff. I never corrected the notebooks. I never looked over their shoulders. Did they save their notebooks? I hoped they did. Mike Marks said he did and marveled at the contrast when his own kid was a fourth a grader.

A Local Field Trip

Dwight led us on a one-block walking field trip to his dad's small neighborhood Seven-Eleven store. The kids crowded into the store and I positioned myself behind the kids. Dwight took charge of the class. "Have you wondered why we have those mirrors up there? They are angled so we can see shoplifters even when they think they are safe behind the tall shelves." Dwight walked us up and down the aisles, explaining as we followed. The kids listened with respect.

Then Dwight led us out the back door. He grabbed an empty cardboard box and placed it directly in front of himself. Then he counted loud and clear, "One, two, three," as he stamped down hard on the box with both feet. He grinned at us. "See. Did you notice how I can 'take down' an empty cardboard box in three seconds flat?"

That field trip greatly augmented Dwight's prestige with his classmates. But several months later Dwight became morose and went about his schoolwork with a gloomy face. His mother explained, "Dwight's dad has been promoted out of the local store and Dwight is no longer a businessman."

A Field Trip to a Goat

Not many kids ever see where their teacher lives. I was teaching at Vineland School when I planned a field trip to my backyard. As the big yellow school bus pulled into my driveway and disgorged the kids of my class, they looked with avid curiosity at me, and then back again to the house and the big asphalt-covered back yard. I could see the wheels going around in the ten-year-old minds as each kid assessed all the information. They saw the net we could string across the asphalt for tennis or badminton and noticed the white lines outlining the shuffleboard area over the side. They may have noticed the tetherball pole back toward the fruit trees. The bus driver was interested, too, and watched me herd the kids together over to the left, to the tall wire fence, which divided my back yard from my neighbor's.

The goat was a real show-off; I had spoiled her by feeding her often when I came out to garden. She crowded herself against the fence and brayed, "baa-baa" for attention. Marcia, my neighbor, was ready for us. She had tied Nanny goat securely and had placed her stool close to Nanny's side. Marcia smiled at the kids, sat on the stool and went to work with her sheers. We watched the heavy fleece fall to the ground and what had looked like a big goat became much smaller. Then Marcia untied her goat, gave it a friendly pat, and turned back to us. She beckoned the kids forward, and had each kid reach fingers through the fence to accept a piece of the clipped wool. "Better than the most expensive hand lotion in the stores. The lanolin in the wool makes your skin very soft." We rode the bus back to school, each kid feeling his hunk of soft wool. All were very satisfied and all smelled like goat. Lu, the principal, came to hear about our trip. He said his nose had led him to our room.

Book Reports

Reading, in my opinion, is the most important skill to be taught in the lower grades; indeed it is necessary in today's world for survival. I constantly changed techniques. trying to make each kid into a reader.

Sometimes each kid had a reading partner with whom he drilled on new vocabulary words before we read a story. Sometimes we had contests, row by row, to see which row could master all the new vocabulary words first. It was always a team situation. No poor reader had to be exposed.

I stressed reading for fun and taught the kids how to choose easy books. "Open the book, read a page. If there are more than three hard words on a page, get an easier book!" I told them about a former pupil, Charles, who trusted my advice. He checked out easy books and read to his little sister and he gained three year's reading growth in the fourth grade. We kept charts for books read. I knew kids hated writing book reports.

My son Jon complained, "What makes a dippy teacher think because I like to read a book about Captain Hornblower, I want to write a book report about it? That takes all the fun out of reading the book." I agreed with Jon. So, no book reports.

I expected each kid to come to me at recess time and tell me about the book he'd finished, and later fill in the space after his name. Mike Marks, very competitive, went off the chart and on to the bulletin board with books he'd read. Many years later Mike, retired naval officer, was kind enough to write a blurb for the back cover of the book you're holding.

Up On Your Feet

Learning to speak well in public—Oh, how important! Ray kept after me, "Are you getting those kids up on their feet?" I remember how we prayed for God's grace to do the job right Sunday mornings after Ray was elected Sunday School Superintendent in our church. Ray wanted to serve his Lord but he trembled every time he had to get up. He deeply resented his many years of schooling and all the "A" grades, but never any practice in public speaking. In Ray's opinion, his teachers were all failures.

I was very fortunate to have Vicky as my student teacher one year. She had won the Olivia De Havilland high school award for public speaking when she was a junior in Los Gatos High School. She was a vivacious girl and very pretty. She gave us some practical hints: stand tall, have one foot slightly in front of the other, don't worry about your hands (just let them hang), take your time (they will wait for you), look at your audience, smile, take a few deep breaths, speak to that person in the back of the room. Some of the kids came back, years later, to tell us how secure they felt giving reports in high school, thanks to Vicky. While Vicky was teaching I was learning, too. She was a real pro.

Not by the Rules

I worked with what I was and with what I had and, of course, I broke many rules. I warned each class at the beginning of the school year that I was not going to obey all the rules. But I told them my husband had covered me with a million dollar insurance police and so if they had complaints be sure they could afford a million dollar's worth of legal help. I don't think I scared any kid but I did get a healthy respect. If anyone can profit from my ideas, they're very welcome.

Control

Kids learn little of value in the midst of constant confusion. And I knew I could not teach well in a raucous class. I used to plan what I'd do if I got an unmanageable class. I could see myself being challenged. I planned to walk to the windows. If they were closed I'd dramatically slam them open. If they were closed I'd dramatically open them.

But that never happened. I managed to have control most of the time in all my teaching years. Of course, there was usually one kid, or maybe several kids, who wanted to show off to the others. One fifth grade class at old Union School fell into line after I scared a big rowdy ringleader boy. I came close to him, glared him in the eye, and when he braced himself for a slap, I kissed him. Any tough guy can handle a slap but a kiss—no way. The kids all looked on in disbelief, then grinned and turned their attention to the lesson in the textbook. Another day I told a gum-chewing boy to stick it on his nose for a few minutes to remind himself of the rules. In the faculty room we teachers discussed various problems. "What do you do about gum chewing, Edith?" they asked.

"I don't have a problem with gum-chewing. I think the word has gone out. I believe the kids are afraid to try it in my room." Actually, a few had come into the class chewing gum, then realized their danger and removed their gum. I pretended I don't notice.

And then came Rick. I braced myself for him. The other teachers had warned me. Rick had been trouble for teachers from kindergarten and on through the third grade. Before school started I hired Mr. Fuentes, Rick's dad, to put in some cement walkways by the side of the house and Ricky, his son, came along to help his dad. Mrs. Fuentes became my "room mother." She still calls me to talk of olden days. Ricky and I became friends. One recess period Ricky said, "Mrs. Robertson, some kids think it will be fun to put sugar in your gas tank. I'll stay after school and wait them out, and on your way home you need to go to a service station and get a lock for your gas tank." Years later I saw Rick driving an AAA truck, on his way to rescue a stranded motorist.

Ellen, a fifth grade at Union School was a rebel, unhappy at home in a dysfunctional family, and continually disobeying rules. I gave her as much latitude as I could but one day during physical education period, she refused to play baseball. She plunked herself down in the outfield and gazed at the sky, searching for airplanes. "When the world is being ruined by atomic bombs you want me to play some silly game?" Then she told me she was going home.

As she walked away and crossed the road in front of the school, then headed down Dent Street, I debated, "Call for the principal to handle it? Let her go—she'll come back if she doesn't get attention?" Sure enough, half way down the block, she slowed down, and then returned to school. We pretended she had never left the school grounds.

The next year, when I was no longer her teacher, she phoned me, "Mrs. Robertson, I am leaving my home. I cannot stay here any longer. I am on my way to see you." I waited. She lived on Blossom Hill Road about four miles away. Ten minutes later she phoned again, "Mrs. Robertson, I'm getting closer. They are strangers here but they are letting me use their phone. I'll phone you again as I get closer."

That worried me. I phoned the police to get advice and they went to get her before she got into deep trouble. She told me later she had a hard time forgiving me but acknowledged I had acted in her best interest.

Problems varied. Peggy came to school with a black eye and a bruised chin, "Silly me, bumping into a door." The black eye healed but later there were more bruises and this time there were bruises also on her brother. Levada, her third grade teacher, and I finally dragged out the story of the stepfather's abuse and Phil's attempts to defend his sister. Social Services to the rescue. Follow-up? I visited the foster home. I listened to the foster mother suggesting that Peggy was at fault for being so seductive. I cried myself to sleep and asked for God's help. Many problems cannot be handled alone.

WOMAN HATER

Jerry was a woman hater, refused to look at a girl. He pretended he didn't know any girl's name. In reading periods I'd have a girl call on a boy and then the boy had to call on a girl. Jerry halfway followed the game. He'd nod toward a girl to indicate he'd called on her. Jerry was not interested in girls; he was a man's man; he was a hunter. Once he showed me a snap shot of ten or fifteen rabbits he'd killed.

Five years later I saw Jerry holding hands with a girlfriend. Puberty had succeeded when teacher hadn't! Years later, when we Calvary Church seniors toured the coast of Alaska, I visited Jerry in his home in the wooded outskirts of Anchorage. He and his wife Melody served me a venison dinner—the meat out of Jerry's well-stocked freezer. He showed me his van, heavily insulated against the Alaska cold and with guns and provisions for his frequent hunting trips when he'd be gone for days deep into the wilderness. Jerry had always been a hunter. He had graduated from shooting jackrabbits in southern California to shooting elk and deer in Alaska. When he was showing me through his house he paused at the chest of drawers in the bedroom and touched the Bible on top of the dresser. "Given to me by your husband, Ray. Did you know that? He made me promise to read it."

Master Teacher?

Teaching subject matter was no big problem for me. I held the kids to high standards and they usually made great progress. Every class I ever taught advanced at least two grade levels in subject matter. By the time I'd taught ten years I was feeling secure in my ability to help the kids process skills and knowledge. By my nineteenth year I began to feel I really knew how to be a master teacher. However I never reached my goals completely. I could teach a kid to read. I could teach even a reluctant kid to read. I could even teach kids whose parents had had disastrous experiences with former teachers and fought me every step of the way. But I failed in my over-all goal: to make each kid love to read. How very true, that saying, "You can lead a horse to water but you can't make him drink."

Chess, Anyone?

Fourth graders, supposedly come from the third grade, masters of all the addition and subtraction facts through twelve plus twelve, and are all prepared for multiplication and division. But, as Paul Robeson used to sing, "It ain't necessarily true." I set myself to re-teach the math facts, and then go on till each kid had learned the multiplication and division facts, too. After a suitable review I gave times tests to weed out those who needed further drill. I bought musical math records and a hook-up to handle eight sets of headphones. From that time on I gave every Friday period to review math facts. I can still see eight young fourth grade learners seated around a table in the back of the room, headphones on, listening and singing with the syncopated "Seven times eight," pause, "is," pause, "fifty-six."

What were the rest of us doing? We were playing chess. I had bought enough plastic chess sets for the entire class. Some kids brought sets from home because, "My set is nicer to play with."

I taught chess using the overhead projector, the kids following, move by move. In a couple of weeks they were enthusiastically eager to play. Chess was taught in many European schools. Many schools in my district were teaching chess and later I took some Vineland School top players to an interschool tournament at Cambrian High School. Jon went from his class, knowing he'd be beaten (Koltanowski was noted for winning games, even when he played blindfolded) but he was hoping to last a few moves. The entire group of kids (probably between twenty and thirty) sat behind their chessboards, playing each other, getting warmed up before the great Belgian-born master player George Koltanowski came. He was scheduled to go down the tables and play each kid, making move after move.

As I strolled about the auditorium Mike Marks beckoned to me, "Come and play me a game. I need to have my confidence built up. This guy across the table here just beat me. Imagine that! Come on, I'll let you be white. Let's play. I need to regain my confidence."

I thought, "This boy needs a spanking," as I took Mike on, playing slowly—and beat him. "Now will you settle down,

Mike!" I scolded. "You are not the only good chess player in the world. Settle down. Stop being so conceited!"

Then the great Koltanowski arrived. The action was fast. He glanced at a board, made a move, moved on to the next board, made a move and again moved on. Ten seconds a move. On he went. Jon went down in just twenty minutes. So did Mike. What had we expected? We had heard he'd played blindfolded against 34 opponents, winning 24 games and drawing 10. We had to say, *"Win or lose—it was a great experience!"*

Strong Teacher Needed

The principal was talking. "Your pre-fab classrooms will not be ready. You'll have to have both sixth grades in the library. It will be a bit crowded." A bit crowded—what an understatement.

In September 1964, we had a hot spell: 90 degrees and upward. I had been pressured by the big shots of Union School District to transfer from old Union School, where I loved teaching fifth grade, to come teach sixth grade at Vineland School. I later learned I was the only teacher in the district considered strong enough to handle the gang of delinquents that had been allowed to develop at Vineland.

The desks were wall to wall with 73 kids. First year teacher Steve, recently out of the army, headed up the other 6th grade. Someone must have thought a young man might be able to cope with classroom brats.

Steve and I worked out a hurried team-teaching system and set up standards. There was no way we could set up standards for the weather, however. With many hot young bodies in a crowded room we all suffered. We coped with the usual start of the school year: yard duty, staggered reading, faculty meetings, CAT tests, and working out class schedule exchanges. Al, fifth grade teacher, took my class for art while I took his for English.

The 75 desks were so crowded they were almost touching. At night my feet hurt from all the walking I had to do to get around in that huge room. Modern math was a farce as Steve and I struggled to teach base seven. The kids had not learned their fourth grade math facts and they certainly didn't take to base seven.

I gave a few lessons on baseball scoring. To twelve year olds a 50-year-old teacher is truly ancient. The twelve-year-old boys resented an old woman knowing more than they did about baseball scoring.

The temperature soared. Don and Donna, tall good-looking blond French twins, were devastated by the recent sudden death of their dad. Donna became very withdrawn. Don, a handsome boy and a natural leader, became a noisy show-off. His widowed mother made him into the head of the family and asked him each morning if he intended going to school that day. Where was the counselor to help Mrs. Berry with her bereavement? Where were the school psychologists to help with problems?

Finally, October 23rd, we were able to move into the portable classrooms and have separate classes. How delightful, even though a new pupil made my class a large thirty-seven, then another pupil brought my class to thirty-eight.

Brats Since Kindergarten

As Steve and I worked together, exchanging classes for various subjects, I could see why I'd been pressured to come to Vineland. Those were the most undisciplined kids I'd ever known. The principal questioned me once regarding my yelling. I wasn't defiant enough to face him down. I felt like yelling back at him, "You've let that gang develop over the past six years and now you brought me here to solve all your problems with a sweet soft voice?"

The girls in the class, at a critical age, not sure of their role, feeling the difference between male and female, were rather quiet. They identified with me but did not want to go against the boys. I was grateful for the quiet, sweet, brilliant girl, Fern. Seeing some boy had failed again in traffic patrol, Fern would grab the special hat, armband, and traffic pole, and go out to cover the neglected duty. Some boy didn't feel like reporting for duty in the cafeteria? Never mind, Fern did it for him. She took over for others so often I wondered how she managed all the class assignments.

I pulled every trick I knew to keep order. My threat of kissing for misbehavior worked for some of the boys. Twelve year old American boys squirm away from mother's kiss, and they certainly don't want a kiss from a teacher. However, the warning didn't bother French reared Don. After the first shock at such an original punishment he just grinned at me.

Five years after that disastrous year I was in front of my fourth grade class, those unruly twelve-year-olds just a horrible memory. Out of the corner of my eye I saw the door slowly open. There stood a tall handsome blond self-assured young man. It took a while before I recognized him—my old nemesis, Don Barry. He strolled deliberately down the center of the room between rows of desks. I waited. He took his time.

He came directly in front of me, leaned down, took my face in his hands, and kissed me on the forehead. He grinned. "I've been waiting all these years to get even." As my little fourth graders looked on in shock I collapsed in laughter. Don gave a courtly French bow, turned and walked out. I never saw him again.

We had many delightful boys and girls but a disproportionate number of bad apples. In the teachers' room Steve and I heard, "That particular gang has been nothing but trouble from kindergarten and on up through the grades. We've never seen such problem brats. How do you stand them?" So, they had been too much for the previous teachers? And now Steve and I were saddled with the addition of Don, a ringleader, catalyst, and a charming bad apple. No wonder my district had demanded their strongest teacher come.

A Cry for Help

Not every kid was a brat. I spoke with one dad about his son's unusual quietness. "He never takes part in class discussions; he stands at the side of the yard at recess."

"Just leave him alone," Dad advised. "He's still in shock from finding his mother's nude bloody body in the shower after that last terrible earthquake we had in Alaska. The only time he's happy is when he's alone out in the fields, driving our big tractor."

I had trouble relaxing at night, got sleeping pills from Dr. Ness. The year became a blur: kids out of the room for traffic patrol duty, kids out for duty in the cafeteria, kids out for newspaper reporter duty. The door was constantly opening and closing. There was never any five-minute period when I had the entire class in the room. There was never a time when I could make an assignment or announcement and know each kid had the message.

Dr. Ness prescribed Librium pills four times daily for nerves. He took me off thyroid, and then put me back again. During the Christmas break there was a big rainstorm. The new portable classrooms leaked, ruining much of my teaching supplies. Teaching became so difficult I would record in my dairy the special times when I actually had a good day. I had a student named Gary for a brief period at that time — an athlete, and respected by the other students, who liked music. He made the music period a joy for me because he liked to sing, and when he sang, the others sang too. Halfway through the school year, his family moved back to Gary's beloved Okeechobee and the music period collapsed. I finally gave up trying. We no longer had music.

The Continuing Battle

Three of our sixth grade boys vandalized six classrooms. They dumped out the kindergarten fish tanks, letting the fish die, urinated in desks, damaged walls, books, and teachers' supplies. In my room they stole my stopwatch and ruined my collection of spelling tapes. I had put weekly spelling dictation on tape so I could walk up and down the rows as the pupils wrote. I would mark with a "C" each well-done sentence, thus encouraging proofreading. Each tape represented many hours of my work.

I put in my request in advance for a fourth or fifth grade for the coming year. I began to use harsher treatments on the ringleaders. One day I sent a student named Don to the principal's office, and when he came back smirking in defiance, I sent him again. I gave permanent seats in math and language classes to separate problem kids. By April Steve and I stopped merely requesting support from the principal. We demanded support — and Paul finally spanked three of the toughest kids.

Open House was difficult, as many of the parents who had problem kids wanted to blame the teachers. Parents who haven't had success in handling their few kids are unable to understand why teachers with near forty pupils can't solve problems that have developed over the years. One mother complained, "I know Celeste is a problem but you make it worse because you don't love her." The mother was right. I didn't love Celeste. I was fighting for survival.

May came and I kept going to school, every day braced for trouble. Steve called in sick several times. Was he taking time off to recoup strength for the coming battle?

I was lasting somehow until noon, then taking a tranquilizer to get me through the afternoon. My faith was weak. I never thought to ask for prayer support from my Christian friends.

Steve Trout called for a sub, and left for Oregon to be with his dad who had had a heart attack. If I'd been smart I'd have called for a sub also, but I struggled on with an ineffectual substitute and two sixth grade classes out of control.

Then, "Hallelujah! Last day of school!" Any words to sum up that awful year?

Rejoice and be glad.

In the future there's no place to go but up.

Chip and the Pearls

Late in the afternoon on the second day of January, I stood in the front door of our home on Englewood Avenue. "But I can't accept a string of pearls from you, Chip," I protested. I explained the rules about no valuable gifts from students. "They are lovely, but I can't take them."

"Who said they're valuable? They're artificially cultured. My dad got them in China; no way he can return them." Chip returned to his dad, waiting in the car. "Sorry to be late, but happy late Christmas." Chip and his dad grinned, waved, and drove away.

Friend Sammy

With only twenty-five kids in my 1965 class, I had time to relate to each one. Cathy, Eddie and Sammy Rodriguez tried to get me a free trip by collecting the Mercury News and cutting out the coupons.

One of my favorite memories will always be of little Sammy digging in a neighbor's garbage can to pull up Mercury News so he could cut out the coupon for his favorite teacher. Sammy was the boy considered the worst brat in the school, always in fights. I asked him years later, "Sammy, what was all that schoolyard fighting about? Seems you were always into some fight."

"Oh, teachers don't understand kids," Sam grinned. "It was just a form of sport. Nothing serious." Sammy and I had always been friends. My rule with him had been, "Don't let me see you fighting," and he never did. The fights were always down over the hill or on the way home. The other teachers gave me credit for handling such a bad boy. Actually, Sammy was one of my favorites.

Sammy and his brother Eddie became our friends. For several years they did yard work for me. Later Eddie worked at our office supply store. The two boys came often for yard work and swims and I became well acquainted with their firebrand mother, Marianna. Big sister Cathy worked for me for a year. Sammy loved animals, owned, trained and bred harness horses for years, and later became an official with the Humane Society.

Thirty-three years after that fourth grade year and long after I retired from teaching, when my main interest was gardening, we had an infestation of possums and raccoons in the back yard. They were eating all the goldfish, figs and kiwis and making a mess in the yard. Ken, the gardener, set traps and carried many unwanted animals off to the woods. One day we found an angry skunk in the trap. Neither Ken nor I was brave enough to deal with an infuriated skunk. I thought of friend Sammy at the San Jose Humane Society.

"Help, Sammy!" I told him over the phone, and I explained the situation, "What do I do now?"

"I'll be right over," replied Sammy, and was soon in the driveway. "Here's my skunk controller," he grinned and showed me a huge rolled-up beach towel. He stood away from the cage then, with a quick motion of his arms, he gave the towel a deft throw. It landed over the cage, unrolling to cover the cage.

That old beach towel absorbed the entire enraged skunk's foul smelling liquid. "There, there, baby," Sam crooned as he put the cage into the back of his truck. "I'll find you a nicer home in the woods." The little boy who had robbed garbage cans to get newspapers for his favorite teacher was now a man over forty years old, but still willing to help his teacher.

Sammy kept in touch through the years. In 2004 he came to tell me of how he rescued a man. The man was trying to commit suicide and Sammy was the first official to get to the school jungle gym to cut down the man who had tried to hang himself.

"We learn how to rescue would-be suicides, but one man to do mouth-to-mouth to another man—I was sure glad to see the guys from the fire department come to relieve me."

Teacher Effectiveness

I was 54 years old in 1968, when I started my 13th year of teaching at Vineland. As I sift through the mass of material (grade book, lesson plans, old "Focus on Fourth" booklet put out by the students) I have many happy memories. What a delightful group of nine-going-on-ten young ones.

Notes from our FOCUS ON THE FOURTH newsletter, comments written by the pupils: Keith: I lead the flag salute and I have to wait for everyone but still be on time. Chris: Joe is in charge of quiet time. It lasts one minute in the morning and after we come in from lunch it lasts a half-minute. Robin: Four rooms have no room mothers yet. It is very hard to find them. We need room mothers to help with parties. Andy: The notebook is 45 cents. Every day we write in it. It has 120 pages in it. You could keep it for the rest of your life if you wanted to.

Ray ordered the hard cover books at a huge discount. My idea was to have the children able to see their progress in spelling, penmanship, and writing ability as they progressed through the fourth grade. Years later students visited, "That notebook is concrete evidence of many fond memories."

And I have fond memories of those precious kids. One close-knit trio of boys, fine students, stayed friends with each other and with me for years. All three were fine students. Keith Garner, a good looking boy, a great athlete, was being reared by his widowed mother in strict Baptist theology; Steve Whitney, slight build, blond, and very shy, had little ability in sports but had inherited his mother's art ability; Barry Rhein, stocky build, a shock of hair over his eyes, a Jewish go-getter, was the ring leader of the trio.

Four years later, in the eighth grade at Dartmouth Middle School, Barry organized a group of teacher assistants working for extra credit. The trio confronted me at Vineland School. "We came to help with your P.E. class, because," Barry explained. "You sure need help in sports."

Steve became the manager of a California chain of bookstores. Keith moved east and we lost him. Barry developed his own business, giving lectures to big Silicon Valley companies on how to improve their productivity

Fourth Graders Put Out a Newspaper

I've lost all contact with the girls but a few of the mothers still keep in touch. Further notes from the class newspaper: Jeff: *Recorders are like song flutes. They are $1.50 each. They make a softer sound than song flutes.* Sonia: *I do not know how to read music but I now know what a staff is and a treble clef. A staff is five lines and four spaces on which you write music.* Gary: *I'm the director of the recorder lessons. We are practicing a canon. That is when half the class starts part of the song and then the other half of the class starts part of the song.* David and Robin: *We had chess lessons. Mrs. Robertson taught us in eight days.* Keith: *Mr.*

Jenkins came into the class for observation. Laura and Marla: *We had a gripe session. We talked and talked and kept talking about one thing. We have red tickets to talk. They are fun to use. We used them one at a time to talk about how to keep things to yourself.*

New Almaden Museum

A worthwhile trip was to the New Almaden Museum at the site of the New Almaden Mines (called new because named for Almaden Mines in Spain) Our school bus went about two miles on graveled Almaden Road lined with orchards and a few farm houses. It is now named Almaden Expressway and the area is built up with very expensive homes. Mrs. Perham, the curator, whose maternal ancestors had come with Portola and Anza into California, had lived for some years with the Yokuts-the mother tribe of the Costanoan Indians. She led us into the museum, gave us a slide show of early Indian life, their general living, foods, basketry, stone implements, and the use of cinnabar as a paint pigment. She told us she joined with the Yokuts in making baskets and, after three years, became almost as skillful as a five-year-old Indian girl.

We Helped Win the Civil War

Mrs. Perham told the story of mercury mining, before and during the Civil War days. She led us through the rooms of amazing Indian and cinnabar mining artifacts. Each kid got to hold a heavy glass jar containing 3-1/2 pounds of cinnabar--86% pure mercury, then, in contrast, another very light weight jar with residue after the mercury had been reduced. She informed us of the many uses of mercury and told how the mining of mercury in this area influenced the outcome of the Civil War. Because the North controlled the mercury and the mercury was used to get gold out of crushed rocks, the North had a vast supply of money to finance their side of the conflict.

GOING IN DIFFERENT DIRECTIONS

In between arguments over finances we were happily married. We made many trips to our trailer home in the gold country and had many visits from relatives.

We had lots of visitors to share our backyard swimming pool. In July I noted that my nephew Mark Conner was perfecting his dive, his brother Matt was trying everything, Mitch and David were timid, Stephen was swimming with his head out of water.

For several weekends we again took a few of my pupils to the gold country. I bought Ray a gold nugget ring to say thank-you for his good-natured putting up with the kids.

I bought Ray twelve Giant Candlestick baseball tickets for his birthday. We attended many games, listened to many during baseball season. June 9th we saw a San Francisco-Mets double header at Candlestick,

I took a summer session class on teaching the recorder at San Jose State—was put in a special section for those needing extra help. Glen was promoted by the Rehabilitation Mental Health to head of the teenage halfway house called Adolescent Rehabilitation Center (or more commonly, just ARC), with a staff of four under him.

At a "Teacher Effectiveness Class" the survey I took said I was moderately authoritarian. When I told Ray, he said, "Ha!"

In 1969 Richard Nixon was inaugurated as the 37th President of the U.S. and hundreds of thousands of people demonstrated against the war in Vietnam. Apollo 11 landed a lunar module on the moon, and Neil Armstrong stepped out onto the surface. Trouser outfits become acceptable for everyday wear for women.

Charles Manson and some of his commune, high on drugs, went on an awful killing rampage in Los Angeles. One of our former Lone Hill students was involved in the Manson murders. I corresponded with her for several years. She's in jail for life. She became a Christian in jail, wrote a book, "Child of Satan, Child of God." She told me the reason she became attached to Manson was that he gave her the love and attention she had never received in school or at home.

I wondered what we teachers could have done to prevent her becoming a Manson acolyte. Her statement made me change my teaching methods somewhat. I resolved to give as much attention to the quiet well-behaved kids as to the brilliant or naughty kids.

I started my fourteenth year of teaching fourth grade at Vineland. We had a great "field trip" to Dwight's dad's 7-11 Store. Dwight, his dad's helper, took us all around, explained how the mirrors show when someone is stealing, demonstrated to us how to knock down empty boxes. The kids were very impressed. They saw Dwight was a real businessman.

Several months later Dwight became depressed. He didn't do his homework. He was no longer alert in school. He stood around at recess, didn't join the other kids in kickball or foursquare. I talked with his parents. Dwight's dad had been promoted and the 7-11 store had another manager. Dwight was now just another school kid.

In the field near our school a two-year old girl was killed, stabbed, and had her throat slit. People were very alarmed, big brothers walked sisters home after school. The murderer was never found.

My student teacher from San Jose State was helpful. Recorder lessons went well. We had a great art lesson when we made Christmas trees from the huge sugar pine cones I brought from the Ponderosa.

That class—a bunch of innocents. Some of their work was so awful it was funny. The kids were delightful but not good students. I tried to bring them up to standard, gave rewards for work done, detention for the others, frequent swims at our pool, had some to the Ponderosa for work and play.

Terri lost part of a middle finger when Chris slammed the door on her. Fast work by Mildred, the school secretary, who got the severed finger, saved it for the doctor to sew on. The kids were very subdued, the teachers depressed. It is always a teacher's fault when kids tangle.

We had a great turn-out for Open House. Over 40 came and the kids shone as they manned their stations for the "Dime-a-Dip."

The end of school came with its usual movie and treats and swimming party, faculty meetings, and then the start of work on the new class assignment. ✍

A Friday in the Life of Edith
October 8, 1999

The alarm goes off at 6:15 am. I get up, turn off the alarm and stretch. I remind myself," *This is the day that the Lord has made. I will rejoice and be glad in it.*" I think of my friend Marge, not expected to live. I pray God will give her a graceful move to heaven. I do a few stretching exercises, my mouth and my shoulders. Bathroom.

6:52   Make bed, dress in clothes I'd laid out last night.

6:58   I take my purse and the latest book I've been reading (M. Gurian's *The Wonder of Boys*) to the kitchen.

7:01   I apply make up (foundation, powder, rouge) and listen to radio news about the Kosevo mess and lawsuits against Germany's government.

7:03   I get out my little 3-pound bar bells and the posture stick for exercising. I turn on television and plug in Stormie Ormartian's *First Step Workout Video*. I start the exercises, thinking fondly of how Christa, 7, and Tabitha, 5, used to exercise with me ten years ago. The exercises start with simple stretches, go on to walking, then to using the barbells. I'm not able to do the weight-lifting parts well but I do the best I can. I finally finish with a cool down part.

7:39 I rewind the video, grab my jacket, and go out front to bring in the recycle bins. I notice some weeds growing, hoe for a few minutes, then come in and write Ken a note about the weeds needing his attention.

7:50 I fix breakfast: 5 almonds, mixed whole grain cereal, sliced banana, skim milk, vitamins, minerals, thyroid, Premarin.

7:59 I eat, reading my book as I eat.

8:10 I clean my teeth. I use tooth bleaching toothpaste, my new ultrasonic toothbrush, another brush for my partial, two other toothbrushes and then my water pic to finish the job. Too bad I had to wait until my teeth are half gone before I take good care of them.

8:22 Clean the sink. Use bathroom.

8:25 Write anther note to Ken, grab my book, lock the house, get the Volvo out on the driveway. I take time to clean the windshield. As usual, I have trouble backing out of that angled driveway.

8:26 I drive to Los Gatos Christian Church where I give my Monday through Friday mornings to being a reading aide in the first grade of the private church school. I drive north on my street, Englewood Avenue, one block. I turn right on Shannon, left on Short Road, right on Blossom Hill Road, right on Camden. I listen to a Christian radio station talking about prayer and fasting, and *God loves you right where you are but* He *loves you enough to want you not to stay where you are.* I turn right on to Hicks Road and park in the church front parking lot. The 9.7 miles had no traffic issues so I arrive early.

8:45 I read more of my present book, *The Wonder of Boys*. The author says boys need 20-30 people outside his immediate family for his on-going development. He should find these people in relatives, church, school, and sports.

8:55 I go up the eight, then the nine stone steps, I fall, skin my hand a bit. I quietly enter the classroom, circle around to the teacher's desk and put my purse away. Janet Brisbin is completing a math lesson; the kids are helping each other put away flash cards. One boy asks when he can get harder cards. Joy to a teacher's heart.

9:05 Janet dismisses a third of the kids to Miss Schneider's class then another group to Mrs. Primeau's class. Then fourteen kids come in for Janet's reading class. A few kids were out of uniform, a treat they earned by bringing back a paper from home. Adam falls as he was rocking back in his chair. He rights himself then begins to wave his reading folder in the face of the girl on his left. He sits on the edge of his chair, falls again, and then rights himself. Albert wanders around then finally sits at his place. Janet Brisbin walks around the room and collects the homework papers. Those who had their homework papers signed are given a sticker, seven boys who had not returned their homework papers are told to lose five minutes of their recess.

The teacher demonstrates, explained the formation of upper and lower case G and H, then Janet and I walk about and help the children do their papers. They are to trace the letters, make five good ones of their own, circle their best letter, then label and color the pictures (<u>gate</u> for G, <u>hammer</u> for H, etc.).

9:15 Janet sends four slow workers into the side room with me to finish their papers. Jake stays longer because he has make-up work due to an absence.

9:31 Jake and I return to the room and I help him catch up with more work he'd missed.

9:45 Recess for the kids. Albert shows he feels very important as he waits to turn off the lights. He is light monitor for the week.

9:50 Janet gives me instructions for the next period. I get my timer, arrange the tables and chairs in the room across the hall, distribute the papers where the kids are to work on the letters J, K, and L. Trip to bathroom. Read a bit.

10:12 Janet sends me the seven girls of the class. I am to try to get Elina to talk. Up to this time, 50 days into the school

year, she has refused to say anything, and I thought it might work if she had only girls around her. I use the timer, tell the girls the first paper has to be done in four minutes. I have each person stand when she's finished her paper. Then the timer goes off and I call, "Ready or not, we will now read the J Book." I turned to the four girls on my right and have them read all the J pages together. Then I turn to the other girls (Elina is in the middle) and have them read the same pages together, aloud. Elina reads with the other two girls! Her voice is soft but she does read! We continue to do the K paper and read the K booklet, then go on to the L work. Elina takes part in each choral reading. I direct the coloring and let the girls share crayons. They enjoy the freedom of helping each other. Two girls decide to color their pictures the same and two other girls also team up. Three girls (Elena is one) decide to work independently. Elina has a very good eye for color and does careful work.

11:45 We were called back to Mrs. Brisbin's class and the kids got ready to return to their home rooms. I got my purse and my book and carefully negotiated those hard stone steps and returned to my car.

11:50 The Volvo was hot, I set all the controls to cool. Once more KFAX on the radio. Will I try to glorify God? How can I find God's will? Hicks Road to Camden, Camden to Blossom Hill. A slow down, some machines doing road work, where there are turning an apricot orchard into a subdivision for luxury homes next to Bob and Shirley's home.

11:05 Home.

11:08 Answer machine is blinking at me. I returned Bob's call, listened about Mary's cancer. Conferenced with

Ken regarding lights to help my sun apartment renter, Laurel, find her way at night.

11:22 Can't read my scribbled notes. Too much was happening too fast. Marge's husband phoned to tell me Marge died two-three hours ago. I expressed sympathy, asked if I could help. Made many phone calls to the church. Pastor Don was out due to his second stroke; others had left for the weekend. I finally got Gary Hess who said he'd take on the job for the church. Marge's grandson phoned, was bewildered at the responsibilities that had fallen on him. I gave sympathy to the relatives and to Marge's husband, all in a muddle. Made phone calls to Edith Randall, the Cheneys, and Barbara Hare.

12:30 Ken and I conferenced regarding the waterfall, talked about placing a phone in the back shed.

12:40 Made out a check for Ken for light fixtures. Entered the check in the ledger, on *Work Order #142—Side and Front Landscaping*. Did some preparation work for the Shepherding gathering.

12:50 Filled three coffeepots. Started to set the tables.

1:10 Fixed and ate lunch: beef patty on English muffin, apple crisp, ice cream. Read while eating.

1:55 More Shepherding set up. Table and chairs from party shed.

2:55 Ken brought in the heavy Sun Harmony Chi Machine which had been delivered by UPS. He unpacked it for me. I tried it out for two minutes. It makes the whole body undulate like a fish swimming, supposedly doing wonders for the entire system.

3:45 To the Dickerson's house with some papers which may help the grandson as he takes on the unfamiliar duties of working through Marge's affairs. Back to do more work for the Shepherding party.

4:30 Phoned Jon, read him part of his mail.

5:00 Rested, used the Chi machine.

5:37 Fixed ice for Shepherding, started coffee and hot water pots.

5:50 Becky phoned. Can't come, will bring salad. I read about the Chi machine.

6:05 Becky came with salad.

6:16 People started to come. Shepherding meeting, 16 this time. Missionaries, Allen and Rosalie, talked about their life and work in Russia. Good fellowship, good food. Shirley brought salad, banana cream pie, pretty harvest theme napkins. She always takes more than her share of responsibility. Everyone helped put things away, did the dishes.

10:00 Everyone gone, late leaving, as usual. I put things away, did a laundry (towels, table cloths, and some of my personal laundry). Cleaned spots off the carpet.

10:54 Read the paper (David shares his with me) while clothes were in dryer. Ate a couple of Asian pears.

11:45 I took the clothes out of dryer. Washed my face. Cut out a news item for Vicky about cleaning.

11:46 To bed. Listened to tape recorder on my headboard. At present it is tape #8 of the Bible, Old Testament. Deuteronomy. Lots of rules for the Jews as they were getting ready to go into the Promised Land. Rules about being holy, obeying God, caring for the poor.

12:41 Too much happened today. I couldn't unwind, so I put on Tape #9, more of God's admonitions to the Jews in the book of Deuteronomy. Still unable to sleep. I finally took a half Valium and conked out. I thank God for Valium. And I thank God for a sensible doctor. Dr. Caton trusts me not to over-dose on Valium. The prescription she gave me for 30 tablets is dated May 1997, and in over two years I have taken less than half. ✍

My Kind of Teaching

Back in 1971 the U.S. had 205 million people, 85 per square mile. China had 760 million people, 305 per square mile. India had 550 million, 655 per square mile. U.S. was conducting large-scale bombing raids against North Vietnam. The 26th Amendment allowed 18-year-olds to vote.

I got out the old lesson plan book for my teaching year. At the top of each page I had penciled times for all the subjects and recess breaks. In the squares I'd put my lesson plans for each period. Scribbled notes in red reminded me that recess duty changed to 10:15, I must get Sam and Ed to move stuff, plan a science unit on light, the library time changed, the Columbus film was coming later.

I find pictures of the teaching staff. Phyllis is wearing a pants suit. Trousers had just recently found fashion approval for women. All the other women teachers are wearing skirts a speck above their knees. There's tall Vern in the back row. Vern died years ago. There's the sweet low-voiced Laura.

Cancer took Laura. Al, with his big mustache, is in the middle row. We often exchanged classes. He'd take my kids for physical education or art and I'd take his for language arts. The last time I phoned him his brother answered the phone. Al had leukemia, could not talk long. I went to his funeral May 15, 2002.

Phyllis is dead, Vern Rose is gone. Big good-looking Hawaiian Lu with his mop of thick dark hair is a retired white-haired gentleman, but still huge and still movie star good looking. I see my middle aged self, my hair dyed a chestnut brown. I had a few wrinkles but my chin was firm, my blue eyes looked out in a confident way.

I study the group picture of the twenty-seven fourth grade kids. There's the pretty little girl, who could read her twin sister's mind, "And so it's not fair to have them both on the same basketball team. They can throw the ball without looking."

There's show-off Robert who liked to display his knowledge of naughty words. "After you," he would say with a low bow, "Please go first, my good pervert friend." Beside him is Dave who excelled in baseball.

The social studies unit was on California, of course. In my old plan book I find a blank California map. I had listed 31 place names in the right margin. I was expecting the kids to place thirteen rivers and eighteen reservoirs and lakes in their proper locations. Later I'd have them learn to locate cities, deserts, canals, mountains, and ranges. We'd put the "before" and "after" maps on display at each quarter. The kids giggled at how little they knew when school started and felt smug at how much they now knew. I heard one dad at Open House looking at the displays, "My kid knows more about California than I do."

And what was going on in the Robertson family in 1971? Ray and I had been married 34 years. Son Jon was 21. Ray's store, Los Gatos Office Equipment and Supply, was keeping Ray very busy. Daughter Sheri came sometimes to get business advice from Ray regarding her family's new office equipment store in Campbell. We had the four grandchildren from time to time, both at our place, where they enjoyed the pool, and at the Volcano place where they roamed the woods and creek.

Ray and I went often to the big double mobile home we had put on the twenty acres on the Pioneer-Volcano Road outside Jackson. Ray called it The Ponderosa. I liked picking the wild blackberries. We went hiking up and down the hills, strolled by the little creek, and walked down the pathways still there—the level places that had been made by the gold miners for their hydraulic equipment.

I remember the soothing sound of water in the creek, creating calm for the soul. Ray said, "It is our restful times here that gives me life to continue on. I think I may live to a ripe old age, after all." Getting away from business problems and family troubles was a blessing. I, too, was content to forget my lesson plans, to have a lull in my teacher concerns.

Many friends, relatives and school kids visited us at the Ponderosa. We often took side trips to various Gold Rush towns such as Columbia, Sonora, Pine Grove, and Jackson where we investigated all the museums, Indian Grinding Rocks, tailing wheels, hydraulic scenes, water wheels, and Daffodil Hill.

Ray and I often visited San Francisco Candlestick Park to watch the Giants. June 6th they split a double header with Philadelphia, the second game going into twelve innings, a homerun by Willie Mays meaning the final victory.*

Every teacher has a special style. Once a visiting young mother came to my room after school and said, "When I heard there was a teacher at Vineland School who taught baseball scoring in physical education, taught chess in math, had junior-high kids as aides, played Screwy-Louie in rainy days, and gave swimming parties as treats for good behavior I just knew it had to be my old teacher from Santa Clara. So I came to see for myself. And I was right, of course. Hello, Mrs. Robertson!" ✍

Jon's Note: Willie Mays—what an incredible baseball player. We often went to Giants games at Candelstick Park, and I remember once watching Willie Mays out in center field waiting as a high fly ball flew through the air, right towards him. At the last moment he turned around, and caught the ball *with his back to home plate.* Magic.

Vineland Gathering

Saturday, January 17, 2004 Jeanette Gilbeau and I went to the grand opening of the new Vineland Library built on the grounds that used to house the Vineland School Kindergarten. Many others had the same idea. We were early but found the traffic was dense; police were there to control the crowd of about a thousand. Jeanette found a parking place not too many blocks away and we joined the group gathered in front of the library. Men and women hurried; kids on the run dodged in and out. We walked past the million dollar homes built where once had been the Mirassou Winery and our Vineland School.

"Remember when we visited the winery and saw the mothers of some of our students, busy putting labels on bottles?" Jeanette said.

"And I remember how pleased the mothers were to know we cared enough to visit next door to our school," I replied. "That was back in the 1970's. "

"No wonder the teachers in the other Union School District called us "the Winos," laughed Jeanette.

The library doors were closed and we wedged our way in the mass, trying to find friends. We worked our way over to Lu Jenkins. The twenty-seven years since I left Vineland School had been kind to him. He was still a tall handsome Hawaiian but his thick black hair was now an attractive gray. Susan Tully was there with her soft pleasant smile. Karen Mullaly joined us. (That red headed ball of fire has advanced in the Union School District until she ranks next to the superintendent in power and prestige). Karen took charge of our little Vineland faculty group and we made our way over to the edge of the crowd.

"I wish I could sort out the memories," I said. "I think 1974 was the year I had the third Rodriguez boy, Billy. And Lou Ann Fuentes was in that class. What a sweetheart she was. No wonder, with such a devoted mother."

We shared memories as the speakers droned on. The parents and kids stood patiently, although the loud speakers did not function well. We waited through long speeches. The third speaker lauded the dedicated teachers of Vineland then said, "And Mrs. Robertson is here today."

How had he known I was in the crowd? Why did they choose to mention me? Other teachers were there as was the principal of the school. Were they surprised to know the old gal was still alive though pushing ninety?

That did it! People searched me out, and I heard, "I'm Mrs. So-and-so, you had my boy, such-and-so. Remember me?" We talked for a bit then another fond mother came up and again I was challenged, "Remember me? My girls were in your class." Or sometimes, "You had my kids. Remember Ken and George?" I learned that George now has his PHD. Erin runs a counseling service in New Jersey.

Several adults, well into their forties, came up and identified themselves as former pupils. One was now a policeman, very trim and good-looking in his uniform. Terry Phillip was a tall lean man, as handsome and self-assured as he had been as a sixth grader. He spoke briefly of his work in Russia and France. Marie Piexoto reminded me how we used to have differences. I remembered that last name with a ch sound spelled with an x.

My head was beginning to ache with the pressure of trying to respond gracefully to those friendly people. In the meantime Karen Mullaly had found a photographer and managed to get the Mayor of San Jose to join us for a group picture. My mind went back to the early days when I came to Union school district. I remembered how I had come to teach In the Union School district.

The day after he was hired to be principal of the new Lone Hill School of Union District, Woody came to my fourth grade classroom door. That six foot four guy could be very persuasive. "Come on and go with me, Edith. I'd like to have a friend on staff. And think how much closer you'll be to home. No more commuting."

I had signed a contract renewal with Arthur Bubb for the fourth grade at Haman School in Santa Clara, but Haman's teaching Vice Principal, Woody Linn, helped me change my mind.

I knew Union District, adjoining Los Gatos, was a "bedroom" community with little industry. My salary there would be less than the California average. I wouldn't have all the extra equipment rich industrial Santa Clara lavished on teachers. "Give me a little time to think this thing through, Woody. No one likes to take a cut in salary. I had better balance the advantages against the losses."

"Who needs time to think?" Woody said. "Only ten minutes to school every day! No commute traffic. Only ten minutes to get home. That means over an hour a day saved!"

I didn't need Woody to do the math to figure the hours saved in a year's time, much less the many months saved in twenty years. I had to laugh at his coaxing. That guy could have been a politician.

My hiring interview next week with the Union District Superintendent was a simple joke, an illustration of "It's not what you know, it's who you know." Woody had already made the arrangements for hiring me. A cup of coffee, a few minute's pleasant conversation, a signed contract.

Finally the doors of the library opened. We stood and watched little kids dodge around their parents to hurry inside. Then the mothers and fathers, on good behavior but in a hurry, crowded through the doors. What a delight! The library is generous in size with lots of room to move around in. It is beautifully arranged, light and cheery with many large windows. There is a fireplace, a special teens' section, many computers, and a large area with undersized furniture for small fry.

Rack after rack of books. Books, books, and still more books, over 125,000, all spanking new. What a joy to see the long lines of people filling out applications for library cards. I saw a little pig-tailed girl clutching a large picture book to her chest. A young boy was already well into his choice, a book about astronomy. A long line of quiet contented kids waited patiently to check out armloads of books.

If they have to get rid of a school there's no better replacement than a library.

California Again... and Again... and Again...

The study of California is required for all fourth graders in our state. I must have studied California history when I was in the Cotati fourth grade—way back in 1923. I remember struggling with the Spanish place names in spelling. Miss Duggan took pity on the little Oakie who knew Indian names but not the Spanish ones. She helped me out one day when she saw the puzzled look on my face. She leaned over to me and whispered *"It's 'San Ho-zay'."*

We studied in school about the early Indians, the Spanish exploration, the days of the missions, the short era of Mexico and of the Gold Rush. It was all fairly vague to me and only moderately interesting.

When I was a freshman at San Francisco State Teachers College I once more studied about our state when I was in a required class on California. Little sister Dorothea, twelve years my junior, was in the fourth grade, also taking the required study of California.

My class was typical college stuff: required text book reading, lectures by the professor, some slides, a little outside reading, some tests. It was a bit humdrum, and again, only moderately interesting.

Dorothea had a gifted, creative teacher with the nerve to crowd all her thirty-some fourth graders into one half of their classroom and use the other half of the floor space for a huge base relief paper mache map of California.

I read about Mt. Whitney, the tallest peak in the contiguous states. When I went home one weekend, Dorothea told me, "Isn't it fun to make paper mache? The best part is mixing in the paste. I got to do Mt. Whitney today. Miss Dartmore told me I got it too high. I had to do it all over. I found out it's high, but not that high. Molly got to do Mount Shasta. It's almost as high." Dorothea was one up on her big sis, on that bit of information. From my reading I'd been under the impression of Mt. Whitney being so high it stood above all the other mountains.

At State College I read about the missions. Dorothea and her fourth grade friends labeled the proper places on their huge floor map for each mission.

At State I studied about Death Valley. I got a rough idea of its location. Dorothea, however, helped scrape the exact area on their map and paint it brown to indicate that it was below sea level.

At State we had periodic tests to see if we could regurgitate the information given us by the prof. In the fourth grade Dorothea and her classmates played a game called *"Who Can Show"* as they took pointers and raced to locate mountain ranges, rivers, lakes, and cities. "It's easy to find the Klamath

Mountains. I just remind myself that clams live in water," said Dorothea.

The years passed. In 1956, nineteen years after I received my life-time teacher's certificate, Jon entered kindergarten. "At last I can get out of the house," I said. "I'd better take a few classes at San Jose State to upgrade my teaching skills." Finally I was ready. I took a job teaching fourth grade in Hamon School in Santa Clara. And once more I was deep into the study of California.

I never had the nerve to duplicate Dorothea's teacher. How did she maintain discipline with over thirty kids crammed close together? I was, however, smart enough to copy many of her ideas. I had each kid make a paper mache California map on a sheet of plywood. Each map was individualized. Some pupils labeled the mountains, some labeled the rivers, some the lakes and reservoirs, some showed the missions, some the cities, some the 49er routes into the state. As the school year progressed the maps became more detailed.

At the beginning of the school year I gave each pupil a blank map and a library book. "Put everything you know on the map and then quietly read until your classmates are through." At the end of each quarter I'd pass out the blank California maps and repeat my instructions, "Put what you know on the map." The kids' early maps often had Alaska as our northern border, the Atlantic Ocean on the west. At the end of the first quarter the kids were proud to see their progress. One boy exclaimed, "Boy, was I mixed up on Mexico on that first map.".

I taught fourth grade for about ten years. Younger sister Dorothea grew up, went to college, and then she, too, became a teacher. Over the years we traded teacher knowledge, compared teaching techniques. Sometimes we took postgraduate classes together.

Once Dorothea and I took a two-week course in the California Gold Rush, and Ray, my history buff husband, chose to audit the classes. We stayed at our trailer on the county Pioneer-Volcano Road. We visited the big hydraulic wheels of Jackson; the Monitor canon which had helped save the North's gold during the Civil War; the Indian Grinding Rocks; Sutter's Saw Mill. We explored the gold rush towns of Columbia, San Andreas, Jackson, and Whiskey Flat. We settled down on wooden benches for class lectures and slide shows in an old hall in little historic Volcano.

We relaxed over lunch daily at the famous Volcano Hotel restaurant: An old cardboard menu was at each table. It simply said, "You eat whatever the cook decides you need." We might have chicken and dumplings or cornbread and lima beans. As we reviewed out notes in the evening Ray, with his superior memory and command of numbers, often helped clarify any questions about dates that Dorothea and I had about the various events in California history.

At the end of the two weeks Ray and I packed up for our return to Los Gatos, and Dorothea got ready to go back to Mill Valley. Big Sis and Little Sis hugged our farewells and Dorothea giggled, " How long have we been doing this California thing? About thirty years? Don't you think it's about time to call it quits?" ✍

Me? A Pioneer?

No doubt about it, I was at a unique place and time for a teacher. I had a husband who supported me and good principals, such as Woody Linn and Lu Jenkins. When I had failings (such as my lack of musical ability), I had wonderful people like my sister Dorothea to help me out.

And the territory was new. When Gerry Inman and I had a huge class of fourth graders in the Vineland School cafeteria, "team teaching" was a very big deal! We had news reporters standing at the back of the room observing our class. I was the teacher who had a typewriter for each kid, way before computers were invented, a chess set for every two kids. I taught paragraphing outside on the blacktop. My fifth graders played baseball, but they also reported for the sports page of our school newspaper and turned in complex scoring cards.

Yeah, I got lots of compliments on my original teaching methods. The greatest form of praise is imitation and many teachers were following my methods. Woody made me the Guide Teacher for Union District fourth grades. But I also fell flat on my face sometimes; my innovations didn't always work as expected!

I'm told that many of my methods involved the right side of the brain through body movements, making learning easy, quick, and long-lasting. All I knew was that kids *doing stuff* are learning, and that kids *sitting* and *memorizing* for the most part, are not learning. That to me was just common sense. Sitting and memorizing a bunch of stuff is painfully boring and you don't actually learn much, but put enough action into the mix and suddenly the classroom becomes a fun place, full of learning and laughter.

At age 93 I can smile and remember when... ✍

www.ingramcontent.com/pod-product-compliance
Lightning Source LLC
Chambersburg PA
CBHW051805040426
42446CB00007B/521